Igor Nemtsev

The Elshad System

MONGOOSE
Press

BOSTON

© 2017 Igor Nemtsev

All rights reserved. No part of this book may be reproduced or transmitted in any form by any means, electronic or mechanical, including photocopying, recording, or by an information storage and retrieval system, without written permission from the Publisher.

Publisher: Mongoose Press
1005 Boylston Street, Suite 324
Newton Highlands, MA 02461
info@mongoosepress.com
www.MongoosePress.com

ISBN: 978-1-936277-82-7
Library of Congress Control Number: 2017907840

Distributed to the trade by National Book Network
custserv@nbnbooks.com, 800-462-6420
For all other sales inquiries please contact the Publisher.

Layout: Stanislav Makarov
Editor: Jorge Amador
Cover Design: Alexander Krivenda
Printed in the United States of America

First English edition
0 9 8 7 6 5 4 3 2 1

Contents

Chess Mirrors Life

I am firmly convinced that life teaches us many rules that are applicable to chess. In life, people have lots of professions and spheres of activity. Ideally, every person chooses a sphere of activity for himself using two basic criteria – what appeals to him, and how much his work will earn him there. Other criteria also apply, but these are more individual and secondary in nature. A person may abandon an occupation he likes, if it doesn't profit him; in so doing, he will acquire the energy and time to pursue a different line of work. In the same way, he may abandon a high-paying line of work or business, if it is in clear conflict with his inner peace. Each of us tries to find this balance between internal satisfaction and prosperity, and the faster we find it, the better. They say that the ideal occupation is the high-paying hobby.

It's the same with chess. Every chessplayer tries to play not only what he likes, but also what puts points on the crosstable. There are two extremes: one brings us into a world of dry pragmatism, where winning is the main or even the only thing; while the other leads us into a world of illusion, where you play whatever you like. Both of these extremes are dangerous to chess in the long run.

In his short, though fiery, chess career, your humble servant has played every variation from A00 to E99, trying to find his own balance. And I can proudly state that I have found it – something that I wish for everyone who sits at the board...

There *is* one little "but" – which also comes from life! When I was young, many parents tried to give their children over to football, or tennis, or swimming, or chess, or sewing, etc., as possibilities to develop the youngster. Each parent tries to develop his or her own child as much as possible, even if it won't help the child very much later on, since he should grow up to be a multi-faceted, well-rounded person. Trainers ought to do the same thing with their pupils. I'm glad that I had such a trainer, who instilled in me the desire to play the King's Gambit, Evans Gambit, Two Knights' Defense, Chigorin's

Defense, etc. Later, we moved on to the "half-open" games. And in 2004, my sizzling romance with the Scandinavian Defense began! But every opening helped to develop my chess consciousness only to a certain level, and then it would be forgotten – still, however, leaving its impression on my play. Don't be afraid to study something new, even if it's "not your style," as it's long been shown that intuition is better developed in players who have studied a wider variety of patterns. This is the way of champions!

Vladimir Grabinsky, one of the best trainers around today, taught his pupils 1.e4 c5 2.b4!? to develop their imagination, and it bore fruit. The so-called chess "byways" don't need to become the main openings in your repertoire, but they certainly will make you more versatile as a chessplayer.

As fate would have it, I made the acquaintance of this book's author, Igor Nemtsev, at the 2015 Aeroflot Open. In Moscow, he is an experienced trainer with both the formal (the required specialized diplomas and titles) and the practical (strong students) achievements in his profession. After warm introductions and small talk , in traditional Slavic fashion I was invited to visit: "Igor, whenever you're in Moscow, you really should drop by..." – which reminded me immediately of a line from the 1969 classic Soviet film *The Diamond Arm*: "You can visit us in Kolyma..." Well, "your soldier" is not of noble blood – so of course, I made use of the opportunity; and a week or so after the next tournament, I dropped in on my "uncle."

The conversation immediately turned to the chess pieces over which we had become acquainted! And, as he had promised, his wife had prepared a sumptuous dinner; but even afterward, we never stopped discussing an interesting position. When I saw this fantastic treasure produced by his chess brain for the first time, I was simply bowled over. After half an hour's introduction to the games he'd played with this miracle of nature, I began wondering how I could strengthen it and make it more flexible. When I finally got home to Riga, I started playing it over the ICC, and with very decent results.

In this book you will be shown, in a light, unforced style, the next twist with an Eastern name: the Elshad System. Naturally, this opening is named after its author – a Muscovite veteran and fan of this ancient game. As an enthusiast myself of the philosophical approach to our game, I like the fact that there are those who try to push the boundaries of our understanding of the harmony of chess, as what we have here is, in my view, the most important thing: the battle for space! Here's an opening with soul! I think that in this book, both children and mature chessplayers, regular players as much as titled professionals, can all find something to like.

The main thing is: don't try to refute this or that strategically risky opening, but rather seek to expand the boundaries of chess thought and the harmony of the pieces. At first sight, giving away a lot of tempi might look like utter foolishness; but any committal approach by White will come back to bite him. Don't forget that, however strong the waves might be, they'll break on the cliffs. And one of the fundamental ideas of this system is to set up a cliff on the e5 square!

But I won't say too much about this opening; better to wish you a pleasant journey through the pages of this book.

GM Igor Kovalenko
Moscow 2016

Some Explanations

In this book, the reader will see all kinds of different ratings. How do you differentiate among them? Player ratings on the Chess Planet website are of course much different from ELO ratings. On Chess Planet, my opponents are mostly expert to master in strength, although occasionally you do get grandmasters. For the games played on the Chess.com site, the ratings are completely different. The 2200-2300 level there is at least 2400 USCF. In those games where I haven't given the ratings, it means that either the actual ratings couldn't be determined, or that the games were played in "live" rapid or blitz tournaments. Most of these were played at a time when official ratings for rapid or blitz did not yet exist; therefore, for the game between GM Rinat Jumabayev and Elshad, I wrote just "GM Jumabayev." For cases where the ratings seem low – for example, 2000 on Chess Planet – this means simply that the game was played before the player's rating under their new login rose to match his actual strength.

Most of the games in this book were played at 3-minute blitz online or in "live" blitz; in casual games; or in rapid tournaments. I also present my game with GM Igor Naumkin (Game 65). It was played in a tournament [the 2014 Aeroflot Open, Round 3 – Tr.] featuring a classical time control, with International Master norms available. I also played an outstanding game with GM Mikhail Brodsky on Chess Planet. Of course, I cannot say with 100% certainty, that he was the one I was playing against. But still, it was played in a team tournament, with the official logins.

I present a few games without commentary, in *Chess Informant* style – my point being that these were very interesting games and I'm sure that the reader will find it rewarding to go over them on his own. One could consider them supplemental material.

The overall results of my games with this opening are over-whelmingly favorable. Roughly speaking, I've scored about 80%. I especially recommend this book to players who already know the basics of playing chess – let's say, 1800 USCF or higher.

Naturally, this opening makes a deafening impression – and not just because of its novelty or its unorthodox nature, but also because of how it dares White! Those who absorb the series of important (though not overly complex) principles of play in this opening will, at any rate, have an advantage in any position arising from it, against anyone. Your author is preparing another book on the Elshad – but this time for White! Elshad himself, the system's author, has been using it for no less than 40 years.

I am not asking you – and especially young players – to play the Elshad System exclusively. But, as a way to broaden your chess horizons, this system is a wonderful thing – especially in blitz and rapid chess!

A Note from the Editor

Like the games themselves, the analysis presented in this book is not primarily intended to ascertain ultimate truth. Rather, it serves two other purposes:

1. To showcase the possibilities that Black enjoys (and the dangers that White faces) in this novel system; and

2. To entertain the reader with spectacular examples of fighting chess.

Don't be surprised, then, if you find improvements to both the play and the analysis. The classic advice from the opening theoretician to his readers applies tenfold in this case: please don't take what you read here as gospel truth, but use it only as a starting point for your own investigations!

This is a new opening, whose theory you can contribute to and help to shape. Consider *The Elshad System* a kind of "interactive" book: we invite you to submit improvements to the analysis, as well as any interesting games that you play on either side of the Elshad, for possible inclusion in any new edition of this book. Please e-mail to: ElshadSystem@mongoosepress.com

– JEA

Preface

When the opportunity comes along for you to write and publish a book, after the initial rush of euphoria there comes the realization of the enormous amount of work you will have to do. Should a master be writing a book, anyway? Or is this something only for grandmasters? I've always wanted to write books! At the tender age of 5, I was already eating up all the chess literature I could. It so happened that one of my first books was a volume of selected games by then-World Champion Anatoly Karpov. I remember how my dad, in giving it to me, asked, "Do you want to become Champion of the World?" My answer was short: "Yes!" It's been 40 years since then, and I did not become world champion; I have read not less than a thousand books, some of them several times over. Some I liked a lot; some, I never finished...

The book you are holding in your hands is a tribute to the life of one man, Elshad Mamedov. Life brings people together miraculously. One day in 2011, in Moscow's Sokolniki Park, we got acquainted by the chess tables they have there. Life was going poorly for me at the time; to put it simply, I needed money. Under such conditions, masters (and grandmasters, too, sometimes) often come to the park to play some games for money, with or without odds. And so I sat down, outplaying the local "masters," and here comes a guy with clearly Asiatic features. He offers to play me; I, of course, agree... and the game begins. I have Black.

1.c3

In the park, people are used to chatter. "Hel-lo!" I saw this move, and was taken aback. "What's this?" I asked him. To which I received the mysterious reply, "Are we going to play, or are we going to chat?" Actually, his choice of words was more colorful than "chat"...

1...d5 2.♕a4+

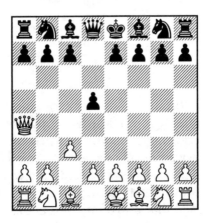

My first reaction to seeing these moves was to laugh; but here's what happened after that: I lost. We played three more games; and at the end the score was 3-1 in the guy's favor. I started making inquiries; and it turned out that his name was Elshad, he played at USCF master level, and he played these sorts of variations all the time.

Now we are friends – practically brothers. And so it's the Elshad System that we'll be talking about in this book.

Introduction

In his outstanding book, *Grandmaster Preparation* (Pergamon Press, 1981), Lev Polugaevsky writes:

> ...I firmly decided to endeavor not to fall into variations prepared by my opponents..., but to spare no time and effort so as to be able myself to set the opponent difficult opening problems as often as possible.
>
> Whether it was this, or something else, that played its part, the role of experimenter became the way for me. And it would be wrong to complain about fate: several times I have managed literally to drag my opponent into forced variations, such that even with maximum ingenuity on his part there has been only one possible outcome. My pregame preparations have enabled me to set my opponent such problems in the opening that he has had no possibility of coping with them at the board. And even if my opponents should say, "It's not worth the trouble. You play hundreds if not thousands of games, and your opening successes can be counted on the fingers of one hand, and besides, they are gained in a strictly limited number of openings," then against them I would merely remind them of an old truth, both in life and in chess: an exceptional moment is worth more than a year serenely lived, or a tournament won. For the reason that, at that moment, the quintessence of creativity, or some part of it very dear to one's heart, can suddenly be concentrated.

The attentive reader will recall that in my childhood I studied the games of Anatoly Karpov. Then there was the after-school chess circle at the Hall of Pioneers, followed by the Physical Culture Institute at Chelyabinsk (Chess Division). I read hundreds of books. Put together, this all gave me a classical chess education. In the periodical press, it was very rare that articles would flash out at me concerning some original setup or such; but on the whole, it was clear to everybody that you had to occupy the center with pawns on e4 and d4, develop your pieces, castle, etc. This is how 99% of people play.

1.d4

This book is devoted to a universal system of play for Black against the closed openings – specifically, against the moves 1.d4, 1.c4, and 1.♘f3. You won't see a strictly instructional opening monograph here. This is an adventure book, surveying the unknown. It's as if you'll find yourself in another galaxy, with four suns circling overhead. Your opponents won't have a single classical guidepost to help them. You will be able to beat anyone you want in a given game. A 2000-level player will be able to beat a grandmaster, if said grandmaster is seeing what's happening on the board for the first time. But I'll give the player with the black pieces a reliable compass. Everything in this book will be, to a great extent, subjective – so we won't be looking too hard for a refutation of the Elshad System. In this opening, White will meet a whole Everest of problems to solve.

And so we begin. When the amateur – and 99% of chessplayers are amateurs – considers what opening to choose against a stronger player, very soon he will start feeling dispirited . Think about it: the master plays 1.d4 against you. If you answer with 1...d5, you'll get a Queen's Gambit position, which is mostly static. A fixed pawn structure in the center gives White the chance to spend the next 100 or so moves squeezing you a little. If you're not playing at the same strength as he is, the likelihood of an unpleasant outcome grows because the master will be stronger than you, he knows the theory better, and he has more experience. What to do, then? You can play the King's Indian Defense or the Grünfeld, but everywhere you turn you're going to run into the same problem: you will have a much better-prepared opponent sitting across from you – from both a theoretical *and* a practical standpoint.

It's only in the Elshad System that you'll be able to say with 98% certainty that your opponent knows *nothing*. He will need to "get creative" right from the start. In this book, you'll see games (even those played at classical time controls) against strong grandmasters, with sad outcomes for them.

1...c6

The system starts, literally, with this move. You may retort that, after 2.e4, we're in the Caro-Kann Defense. First off, though, we can still play Elshad's opening; and secondly, we never said we were refuting 1.d4.

2.c4

The point is that White, having opened with 1.d4, has no intention of swerving from his opening strategy. Why did he play 1.d4? Probably because he much prefers that move to 1.e4. People are basically conservative. If you're all set to play a closed opening, odds are you won't suddenly opt for a Caro-Kann. There are few who can play sharp, open positions just as well as they can play closed openings. So the chance of 2.c4 is great. Well, that's all I have to say – White fell for it! He won't be able to pull his c-pawn back to c3 so that it can support his d4-pawn.

2...d6

This is the first important fork in the road for the Elshad System, whose author himself prefers to play 2...♛a5. This is a continuation we will also examine very closely in this book.

3.e4

Since Black appears to be simply abandoning the center, of course White will seize it! Sometimes a transposition of moves happens – say, 3.♞c3 or 3.♞f3; but it all works out the same eventually: White is going to grab the space, because it's "what you do."

3...♞d7

In this book we will give an explanation for every one of Black's moves. Every idea, any plan will be subjected to careful analysis. Soon we will reach the *tabiya*, the basic position of the entire opening. And so – where is the knight going? The next part of Black's plan involves the moves ...h7-h6, ...g7-g5, ...♗f8-g7, and ...♘d7-f8. Next, this knight will jump out to e6 so that Black can hit the d4-pawn multiple times, inducing White to advance with d4-d5. At that point, the knight goes back to f8. And, since the e5 square now belongs to us, the horse takes a new route: ...♘f8-g6-e5! If you're playing a blitz game, by this point you'll already have gained at least half a minute on the clock. But even in classical chess, as will be shown later, even grandmasters can fail to solve these problems.

4.♘c3 h6

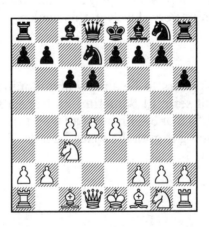

Yet another important fork in the road. White has so many possibilities here!

The most popular lines here start either with 5.f4 or 5.♞f3; these will receive most of our attention. But other moves will not remain shrouded in mystery. Anything that's the least bit dangerous to Black will find illumination in our book.

5.f4

Still, the legitimacy of the creator of this opening is important. This position does not appear on even a single chess database, whereas my own database contains more than a hundred games played by Elshad, by me, or by my students. The system's author himself has been playing this opening since 1975.

5...g5!

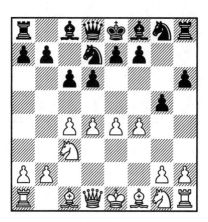

This move is the whole point of the system! Igor Kovalenko, a strong grandmaster, had a most interesting thought when he visited me and reviewed some of the materials for this book: "White," he said, "is simply setting up his game in classical style, and he is unprepared for a concrete, move-by-move game." The grandmaster went on to compare this situation to a classically trained boxer finding himself in a street fight where there's no referee, nobody is stopping the fight, and there's nowhere to run!

6.fxg5

The first thing White can't understand is: what is Black giving the pawn up for?

6...&g7

This recalls one of the ideas in the Volga *[or Benko – Tr.]* Gambit, on the opposite wing. Here the gambit ideas are even stronger, since they are typically directed against White's king.

7.gxh6

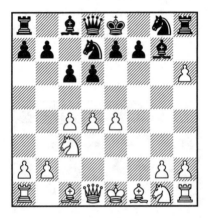

Consistent, at any rate. And so, on to our games.

Chapter 1

The Main Line: White Plays f2-f4

1. Kretschmer – Nemtsev

Elshad System
8/27/2014

1.d4 c6

We must start with exactly this move, since once your opponent opens with 1.d4 he is unlikely to follow up with 2.e4, as that would result in a Caro-Kann; whereas with his opening move he's indicated that he wants to play a closed game.

2.c4 d6

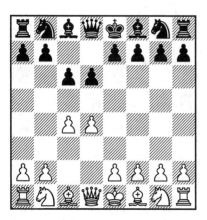

This looks provocative, as it does encourage 3.e4; but for now, White is reluctant to play that.

3.♘c3 ♘d7

But now of course we have to go 4.e4 – after all, isn't that what we've been told our whole lives?

4.e4

But now comes the first problem for White: the d4-pawn is weaker now that it can no longer be protected by pawns (they're standing on e4 and c4). Now Black begins surrounding the d4 square. Still, this intention is not yet obvious, so Black's next move looks like foolishness, or even like he's mocking White's skills. How the first player wants to punish his opponent for this contempt toward the laws of chess!

4...h6

What's this?? How dare Black play this way? What nonsense! Instead of developing pieces, instead of occupying the center with pawns?!

5.f4

He really, really wanted to go there. Now Black can't play ...g7-g5. Or can he?

5...g5 6.fxg5

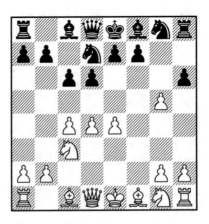

White might still have stepped off the path of doom, while still playing consistently: 6.e5!? ♗g7 7.♘f3 ♘f8 8.exd6 ♕xd6 9.fxg5 hxg5 10.♗xg5 ♘e6 11.♗e3 ♘h6.

6...♗g7 7.gxh6 ♘xh6 8.♘f3

For the player running into this opening for the first time, it still seems as though his opponent is intoxicated; but Black's next move is bound to look like a slap in the face!!

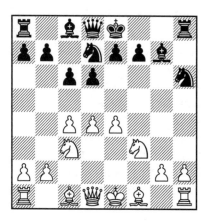

8...♘f8

Since Black's entire strategy in this opening is based on the dark squares, then obviously Black intends to occupy important dark squares, specifically d4 and e5. Those are the most important squares on the whole board right now. But there are also other good moves, such as 8...c5!? and 8...♘g4!?.

9.♗g5

Does White seriously think that Black is going to play ...e7-e5 here, blundering away the queen? Or maybe this is simply developing a piece...

9...♘e6 10.♗e3 ♘g4 11.♕d2

This loses right away, of course, but at any rate Black's advantage is already great enough; while considering what else we know about the system White's chances are by now practically gone. And 11.♗g1 changes nothing.

11...♘xe3 12.♕xe3 ♕b6 13.♖d1

13.♕d2 ♘xd4 14.♘xd4 ♕xd4 15.♕xd4 ♗xd4 16.0-0-0 ♗e5 17.h3 ♗e6 18.♔b1 0-0-0 leads to a very difficult endgame for White – the bishop pair and weak pawns, especially the one on e4.

13...♕xb2 14.♗e2 ♗h6!

The number of queens lost after this bishop maneuver is beyond counting.

15.♕d3 ♘f4 16.♕d2 ♘xg2+ −+

This was an Internet game; immediately after resigning, my opponent wrote me, telling me exactly what he thought of me – and about my parents, all my relatives, how little I knew about the game – and finally, how if we ever met, he would break my arm.

0-1

2. Diplodoc (2507) – Nemtsev_Igor (2741)

02/20/2015

1.d4 c6 2.c4 d6 3.♘c3 ♘d7 4.e4 h6 5.f4 g5 6.fxg5 ♗g7 7.♘f3

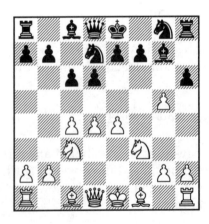

White's not showing himself to be too greedy – yet. Meanwhile, Black is just forging ahead, developing his pieces according to plan. He is aiming at the d4 square.

7...♘f8 8.♗e2 ♘e6

Black would do better to take the pawn with 8...hxg5, transposing into the system's usual lines: 8...hxg5! 9.♗xg5 (9.♘xg5 ♕b6 10.♘f3 ♘e6 11.d5 ♘f8) 9...♘e6 10.♗e3 ♕b6 11.♖b1 (11.d5 ♕xe3) 11...♘h6 12.0-0 ♘g4 13.♕d2 ♘xe3 14.♕xe3 ♘xd4 15.♘xd4 ♗xd4. After the game move, White can play 9.g6 fxg6, with a very confusing position.

9.d5

9.0-0 ♕b6 10.♗e3 hxg5 11.♘xg5 ♘xg5 12.♗xg5 ♗xd4+ 13.♔h1 ♕c5 14.♗d2 ♕e5:

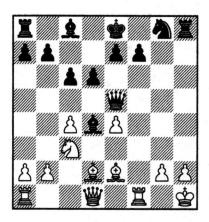

15.♗f4 ♕g7 16.♕d3 e5 17.♗g3 ♘f6 18.♗f2 ♗e6 19.♗xd4 exd4 20.♕xd4 ♖xh2+ 21.♔xh2 ♘g4+ 22.♗xg4 ♕xd4−+.

9.0-0 ♕b6 10.♗e3 ♕xb2; 9.gxh6 ♘xh6 10.0-0 ♕b6 11.♗e3 ♘g4 12.♕d2 ♘xe3 13.♕xe3 ♘xd4 14.♘xd4 ♗xd4.

9...♘c5

9...♘xg5!?:

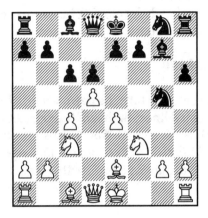

This move is both stronger and more in the spirit of the position, e.g. 10.♘xg5 hxg5 11.♗xg5 ♛b6 12.♛b3 (12.♛d2 ♘h6 13.♗e3 c5 14.h3 ♘g4 15.♗xg4 ♗xg4 16.0-0 ♗xh3 17.gxh3 ♖xh3) 12...♖xh2! 13.♖xh2 ♛g1+ 14.♗f1 ♛xh2∓.

10.♛c2 hxg5 11.♗xg5 a5

11...♛b6 12.♗e3 ♘f6 13.h3 ♘g4 14.♗f4 ♘f2!! 15.♔xf2 ♘d3+ 16.♔g3 ♛f2+ 17.♔h2 ♖xh3#.

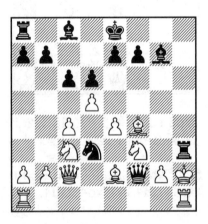

A rather typical mate in the Elshad System – I have gone through it myself. After the sort of nightmare that White would suffer in a blitz match, your opponent might simply give up chess altogether. Or maybe start playing 1.e4 instead. But getting used to playing against this opening during the course of a blitz match is impossible!!

11...♞h6 12.b4 ♞xe4 13.♛xe4 ♝xc3+ 14.♚f2 ♝xa1.

12.0-0 ♞f6 13.a3 a4

This move is not forced. Black can play 13...♛b6 right away, with a powerful attack.

14.♚h1

14.b4 axb3 15.♛d2 ♛b6 16.♝e3 ♞g4 17.♝f4 (17.♝d4 ♝xd4+ 18.♞xd4 ♞xh2; 18...b2 19.♜ab1 ♞b3) 17...♞xe4+.

14...♞g4 15.h3 ♛b6!

Surprise! Turns out the knight wasn't threatened after all. A typical misconception by White in this opening.

16.♜ae1 ♞d7 17.e5 ♞f2+

17...♞dxe5 18.♞xe5 ♞xe5 19.dxc6 bxc6 20.♞xa4 ♛d4 21.♛c3 ♛xc3 22.♞xc3 ♜b8=.

18.♜xf2 ♛xf2

Even though the computer says White has a large advantage here, finding all the right moves over the board is unrealistic – especially if it's a blitz or rapid game. And all the more so when we are playing people and not chess engines.

19.e6 ♞e5 20.♜f1 ♛g3 21.exf7+ ♚f8

Elshad's favorite spot for his king.

22.c5 ♝xh3 23.♝xe7+ ♚xe7 24.cxd6+ ♚d8

White will be mated in not more than four moves.

25.gxh3 ♜xh3+ 26.♞h2 ♛xh2# 0-1

3. Goltzman_Evgeny (2578) – Nemtsev_Igor (2828)

3/28/2015

1.c4 c6 2.♞c3 d6 3.d4 ♞d7 4.e4 h6 5.f4 g5 6.fxg5 ♝g7 7.♞f3 ♞f8

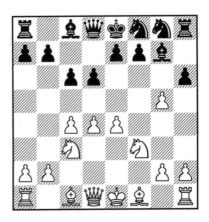

The standard way to handle the position. Nonetheless, Black also has some other interesting solutions. Let's take a look.

7...c5!?:

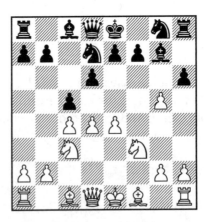

Notice White's pawn structure. If Black takes on d4 – or White hits at c5 himself – then White's pawn chain will look as though he'd had a front tooth knocked out. The dark squares d4, c5, and e5, among others, all give Black opportunities for active play.

8.dxc5 ♘xc5 9.♗e2 hxg5 10.♗xg5:

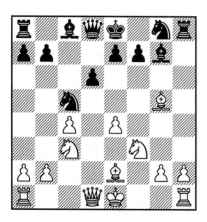

10...♗xc3+! 11.bxc3 ♘xe4 12.♕d4 ♘gf6 13.♗xf6 ♘xf6 14.0-0 ♕a5. Although *Houdini* shows an evaluation of "0.00-0.00" here, nevertheless, White's weak pawns and lack of obvious targets (what's his plan?) give us a basis for preferring Black's chances in the fight ahead.

8.♗e2 hxg5 9.♗xg5 cxd4 10.♘xd4 ♗e5 11.♘f3 ♗xc3+ 12.bxc3 ♕a5 13.0-0 ♘gf6, with tremendous play for Black.

8.d5 hxg5 9.♗xg5 ♕b6 10.♖b1 ♘e5 11.♗e2 ♘xf3+ 12.♗xf3 ♗e5 13.h3 ♘f6 14.0-0 ♖g8 15.♗xf6 exf6 16.♔h1 ♗d7 17.♕d3 0-0-0 18.a3 ♖g3 19.b4:

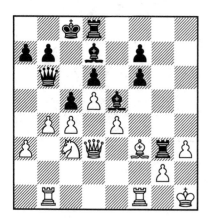

With opposite-side castling, generally the one principle that applies is who's faster.

19...♗xh3 20.gxh3 ♖xh3+ 21.♔g1 ♖g8+ 22.♔f2 cxb4+ 23.♔e1 ♗xc3+, and that's it for White. Not an absolutely forced line; still, it does showcase Black's attacking possibilities.

7...♕b6!?:

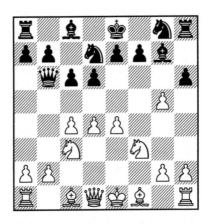

8.gxh6 ♘xh6 9.♗e2 ♘f8 10.0-0 ♘e6 11.♗e3? ♘g4:

White's position is indefensible.

7...hxg5!?:

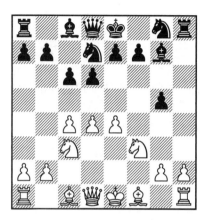

8.♗xg5 ♘f8 9.♗e2 ♘e6 10.♗e3 ♘f6 11.h3 ♘g4:

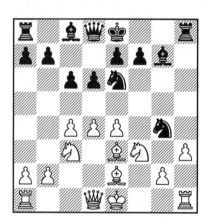

Let's not forget this tactical trick!

12.♗d2 ♕b6 13.d5 ♕f2#:

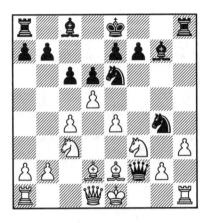

Yegorov – Nemtsev, Internet 2015.

8.♗d3

Not the best move in this position. The problem is that on d3 this bishop stands between the queen and the d4-pawn, depriving the latter of its essential connection to the rest of White's pieces. Also, generally speaking, the bishop isn't too well placed on d3. In principle it belongs among the ranks of poorly placed pieces – for instance, as in similar King's Indian Defense lines.

8...♘e6?!

This is an inaccuracy, giving White an unexpected opportunity.

8...hxg5!:

(see diagram next page)

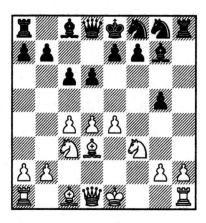

This would be the right choice!

9.♗xg5 ♘e6 10.♗e3 ♘h6.

9.gxh6

9.g6!? ♘xd4 (9...fxg6 10.e5 dxe5 11.♗xg6+ ♔f8 12.dxe5 ♛xd1+
13.♘xd1 h5 14.0-0 ♘h6 15.♘g5+ ♔g8 16.♘f7 ♘xf7 17.♗xf7+ ♔h7
18.♖f5±) 10.gxf7+ ♔xf7 11.♘xd4 ♗xd4 12.♛h5+ ♔g7 13.e5 ♗xe5
14.0-0 ♛b6+ 15.♔h1 ♘f6 16.♛g6+ ♔f8 17.♗xh6+ ♖xh6 18.♛xh6+
♔e8 19.♖ae1±.

9...♘xh6 10.d5 ♘c5!

There is no need to bring the knight back to f8 – the more so,
in that White could disrupt Black's harmony with the breaks e4-e5
or c4-c5.

11.♗c2 ♘g4 12.h3 ♛b6 13.♛e2

This is forced, considering Black's possibility of retreating the
c5-knight followed by mate on f2.

13...a5 14.♖f1 ♘e5 15.♘xe5 ♗xe5 16.♛f3 f6!

A very important resource in many lines: one pawn neutralizes two of White's major pieces on the f-file.

17.b3 a4

17...♖h4!? 18.♗b2 a4 19.0-0-0 axb3 20.axb3 ♘xb3+ 21.♗xb3 ♛xb3 22.♛d3:

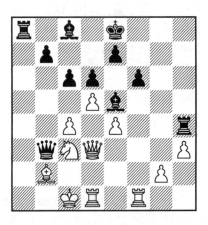

22...♖xe4!! 23.♛xe4 ♗xc3 24.♛g6+ ♔d8 25.♛c2 ♗xb2+ 26.♔d2 ♛g3 27.♛xb2 ♖a2 28.♛xa2 ♛g2+ 29.♔e3 ♛a2−+:

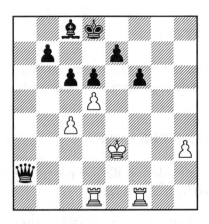

Let's evaluate the respective sides' kings from a safety standpoint. The black king just stays in place, without castling, while White's king gets checkmated.

18.♖b1 axb3 19.axb3 ♛b4

19...♖g8!? 20.b4 ♘d3+ 21.♛xd3 ♖g3 22.♖f3 ♛g1+ 23.♛f1 ♗xc3+ 24.♔d1 ♛xf1+ 25.♖xf1 ♖xg2∓:

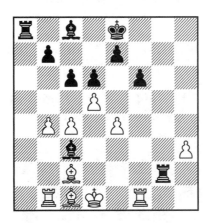

A typical picture – but a sad one for White.

20.♗d2 ♛b6 21.b4 ♘d7 22.dxc6 bxc6 23.b5 ♖a3

23...♗xc3 24.♗xc3 cxb5 25.♖xb5 ♛c7 (25...♛c6!) 26.e5 ♖a3 27.exd6 ♛xc4 28.♗g6+ ♔d8 29.♗a5+ ♖xa5 30.dxe7+ ♔xe7 31.♛e3+ ♘e5 32.♖xa5 ♛b4+ 33.♛d2 ♛xd2+ 34.♔xd2 ♘c4+ 35.♔c3 ♘xa5 36.♗f5 ♗xf5 37.♖xf5 ♘c6 38.♔d3 ♔e6 39.♔e4 ♘e5 40.♖f2 ♖h4+ 41.♔e3 ♖a4 42.♖c2 ♔f5 43.g3 ♖a3+ 44.♔f2 ♘d3+ 45.♔g2 ♘e5 46.♔f2 ♔e4 47.♖e2+ ♔d4 48.♖b2 ♖f3+ 0-1 (Goldman – Nemtsev, Internet).

24.♖b3

24.bxc6 ♛xc6 25.♖b3 ♖a1+ 26.♔e2 ♛xc4+ 27.♛d3 ♛xd3+
28.♗xd3 ♖xf1 29.♔xf1 ♘c5 30.♖b8 ♔f7 31.♗c4+ d5 32.♗xd5+ e6
33.♖b5 ♗a6 34.♗c4 ♗xb5 35.♘xb5 ♘xe4−+.

My opponent, a fairly well-known veteran chessplayer, turned
out to also be a very principled one.

**24...♖xb3 25.♗xb3 ♘c5 26.♗c2 ♗e6 27.bxc6 ♛b2 28.♔d1
♛a1+ 29.♗b1 ♗xc3 30.♗xc3 ♛xb1+ 0-1**

4. VakhramovValik (2689) – Nemtsev_Igor (2639)

3/27/2015

**1.c4 c6 2.♘c3 d6 3.d4 ♘d7 4.e4 h6 5.f4 g5 6.fxg5 ♗g7
7.♘f3 ♘f8 8.gxh6 ♘xh6 9.♗f4 ♘e6 10.♗g3 ♛b6∓**

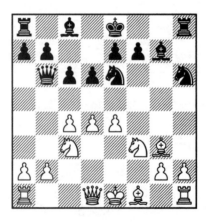

Now both the b2- and d4-pawns are under attack; there is no
way to save them both.

11.♗f2 ♛xb2 12.♖c1 ♘g4 13.♖c2 ♛b4 14.♗g1 ♗h6

14...c5!∓:

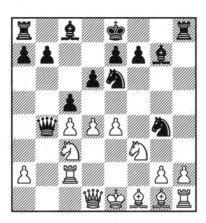

Hitting d4 would have been the most logical conclusion for the struggle – and the quickest, too: 15.h3 &d7 16.&c1 &c8 17.&b3 &xb3 18.axb3 &xd4 19.&xd4 cxd4 20.&e2 &e3 21.&xe3 dxe3–+.

15.&d3 &f4

15...&e3! 16.&xe3 &xe3 17.&e2 &xc2+ 18.&xc2 c5 19.0-0 cxd4 20.&d5 &a3∓.

16.g3 &g2+

16...&h3!.

17.&e2

17.&xg2 &xc3+ 18.&f1 &e3+ 19.&xe3 &xe3, and White's position is very bad.

17...&2e3 18.&b1 &xb1 19.&xb1 &xc2 20.&xc2 &e6 21.&bd2 0-0-0 22.h3 &g7

Remember this trick! White cannot take the piece on g4 due to the pin on the h-file.

23.d5 &d7 24.&xa7 c5 25.a4 &e5 26.a5 &xh3 27.&g1 &xf3 28.&xf3 &g4 29.&e3 &xf3 30.&xf3 &e5 31.&g2 &g8 32.&e2 &gxg3 33.&xg3 &xg3 0-1

5. Chelentano (2483) – Nemtsev_Igor (2490)

1/4/2015

1.d4 c6 2.c4 d6 3.♘c3 ♘d7 4.f4 h6 5.e4 g5 6.f5

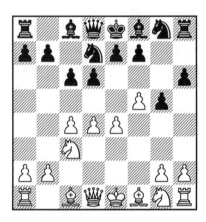

This move cannot aspire to be the best in this position. It would be a big stretch to call it taking space.

Now Black switches plans. To be precise, he doesn't waste time moving the knight to f8, but simply begins a direct assault on d4.

6...♗g7 7.♗e3

7.♘f3?!:

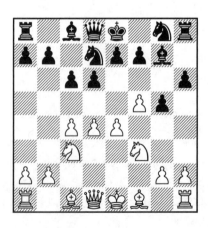

This gives Black the chance to carry out two standard ideas (...g5-g4 and ...c6-c5), both of them aimed at disrupting the d4 point!

7...c5 8.d5 (8.h3 cxd4 9.♘xd4 ♗e5! 10.♗e3 ♗g3+ 11.♗f2 ♗xf2+ 12.♔xf2 ♘gf6 13.♔g1 ♘e5∓) 8...g4 9.♘d2 ♘e5, and White's pawn structure resembles a broken-down fence. If White later castles short, one might execute a direct attack on it with ...h5-h4-h3. And if White castles long, then the typical King's Indian plan of attack, with ...a6-b5 and a powerful attack on the a- and b-files, should work well.

7...♕b6 8.♘ge2

Apparently just hanging a pawn: I can't see any compensation for it.

8.♕d2:

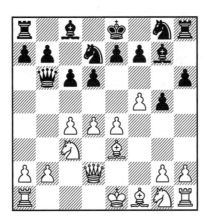

This is a lot stronger. Here it's important for the reader to understand the overall coordination of the pieces in the Elshad System.

8...♘gf6

When White puts his queen on d2 and his bishop on e3, the g8-knight heads immediately for the g4 square, the point being that if we can trade off the e3-bishop, White will have one less defender

Chapter 1

of the d4-pawn, which is the linchpin of his whole position. It's also very important to know that Black need never be afraid of the d4-d5 break. Black, in fact, induces this immediately – for, after d4-d5, Black has two fundamentally different means to wage the coming battle:

1) ...c6-c5, which is just a positional plan of playing on the dark squares. Play in the center is closed, and therefore moves to the wings. And Black has the better of it on both wings. It's also important that Black has no intention of castling; while White, unfamiliar with this system, and having long been classically educated, will feel uncomfortable with his king sitting on e1. He will have a hard time trying to decide where to hide the royal. White's problem is that wherever he goes, somebody will be waiting for him.

2) Reposition his queen to either a5 or c7, with the c6-pawn staying where it is.

8...♛xb2 9.♖b1 ♛a3 10.♖b3 ♛a5∓ 11.g3?!

A useless attempt to reorganize his pieces somehow.

11...♘gf6 12.♗g2 ♘g4

12...♘b6, winning the c4-pawn, is also strong.

13.♗d2 ♛c7

13...♛a6!?.

14.h3 ♘gf6 15.0-0

(see diagram next page)

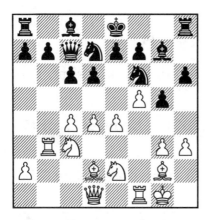

The critical position: Black has a clear advantage, but he needs to find the decisive continuation.

15...h5

Unfortunately, this is where I strayed from the true path. On the other hand, it resulted in an elegant finish, right in the spirit of this opening!

The true path is 15...♘b6! 16.c5 dxc5 17.dxc5 ♘c4! (The idea is not just to seize the key square e5, but also to eliminate the d2-bishop, the defender of the dark squares. Meanwhile, the e5 square could be taken over by Black's other knight!) 18.♖b4 ♘xd2 19.♛xd2 ♘d7!!.

16.♗xg5 b6 17.♖a3 ♖g8

This is a very important move. In many lines in this opening, the rook moves precisely here, grinning from afar at the white king.

18.♘f4 ♗b7 19.♘xh5

The fatal error. I continue to insist that an unprepared opponent will be unable to cope with all the twists and turns of our system over the board.

19...♘xh5 20.♕xh5 ♗xd4+ 21.♔h2 ♘e5 22.f6 e6 23.♘e2 ♗c5 24.♖c3 0-0-0 25.♗f4 ♖h8

The queen is trapped, so White resigns. **0-1**

6. Chelentano (2501) – Nemtsev_Igor (2472)

1/4/2015

1.d4 c6 2.c4 d6 3.♘c3 ♕a5 4.e4 h6 5.f4 g5

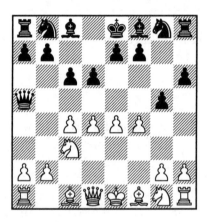

Another basic position in this opening.

6.f5

My opponent seems to have a preference for playing for the squeeze.

6...♗g7 7.♗e3

7.h4!?, hitting the g5-pawn, is a very tempting try. Here too, though, Black has a cute trick: 7...♘f6! (7...g4 is also good for Black – it deters the white knight from coming out to f3 and, if White takes the g4-pawn, then the bishop captures on d4) 8.hxg5 ♘xe4! 9.gxh6 ♗f6 10.♘ge2 ♗xf5, and Black has the initiative.

7...♞f6 8.♗d3

After 8.♞f3, Black jumps his knight to g4 immediately, with a clear advantage.

8...♞bd7 9.♞f3

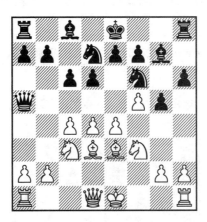

A critical position for this variation. Here, besides the line actually chosen, Black has at least two strong alternatives.

9...♞g4

9...b5! 10.cxb5 cxb5 11.♗xb5 ♞xe4 12.♕d3 ♞xc3 13.bxc3 ♖b8 14.a4 g4 15.♞d2 ♖xb5 16.♕xb5 ♕xc3 17.♔e2 ♗xd4 18.♗xd4 ♕xd4 19.♖ac1 0-0, and White cannot hold.

9...c5!? (striking at the key square without delay) 10.dxc5 ♞xc5, with a powerful initiative on the dark squares for Black. White's center is a shambles.

10.♗g1 c5 11.♞xg5?

A typical grievous blunder from White in this opening. The unusual situations that arise are such that the thread of the position vanishes, and White starts shooting at ghosts.

11...hxg5 12.♕xg4 cxd4

As annotators are wont to say in situations like this, the rest is a matter of technique.

13.♕xg5 ♗f6 14.♕c1 dxc3 15.b3 c2+ 16.♔e2 ♘c5 17.♗e3 ♘xd3 18.♔xd3 b5 19.♕xc2 bxc4 20.bxc4 ♗a6 0-1

7. Tretyakov_Sergei (2457) – MASTER_GURU (2502)

12/31/2013

1.d4 d6 2.c4 c6 3.♘c3 h6 4.e4 ♘d7 5.f4 g5

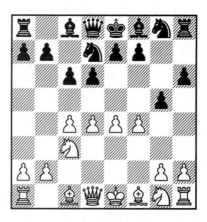

One of the Elshad System's most important positions. Naturally, the most common continuation is 6.fxg5.

I decided to find out what *Houdini* recommends in this position. As it turns out, the engine doesn't even list the capture among its first three lines, suggesting instead 6.e5 and 6.♘f3. The game move below is also a regular guest in my games. The play is then substantially different, although it can often transpose into the preceding games.

6.f5 ♗g7

The d4 square remains critical in this line, too.

7.♘f3 g4!

Simple and strong. The d4-pawn's defender must get pushed off the f3 square; besides this, obviously, White loses time with the knight's wanderings. There is also a concrete way to resolve the dark-square problem: 7....c5!? 8.d5 g4 9.♘d2 ♘e5 10.♗e2 ♘f6 11.0-0 h5:

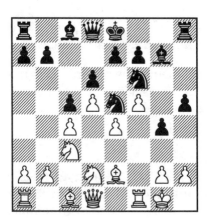

8.♘g1

8.♘d2? simply loses the d4-pawn after 8...♗xd4.

8.♘h4 (the "Tarrasch" knight) 8...♕b6 9.♗e3 ♗f6! 10.g3 ♗xh4 11.gxh4 ♕xb2.

8...h5

As has been said many times before, this move is not completely necessary, since the g4-pawn isn't hanging. If the queen takes it, then the g7-bishop will eat the d4-pawn. Those pawns are not equivalent in value. So it would be quite all right to start playing on the queenside with 8...♕b6, 8...♕a5, or 8...c5.

9.♘ge2

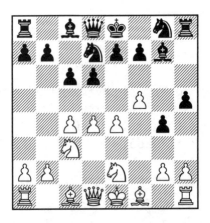

Instead of the following move, here Black has a curious possibility in the spirit of the King's Indian Defense, involving ...a7-a6 followed by ...b7-b5-b4.

9...♕b6

9...a6 10.♗e3 b5 11.c5 b4 12.♘a4 dxc5 (this move has already become standard: any pawn advancing to c5 or e5 must be wiped out at once) 13.dxc5 ♕a5 14.♗d4 ♗f6, with complex, confusing play.

10.g3

Houdini rightly rates this position as favoring Black. Generally speaking, based on my experience in playing this kind of position, I would have to say that this is not the best way to play against Elshad's System.

10...h4! 11.♘a4 ♕a5+

Excellent. In defending himself against the check, White cuts off the natural lines of communication between his queen and the center pawn on d4. But there is also another, unexpected possibility: 11...♕b4+!? 12.♘ac3 ♕xc4∓. Surprisingly, the black queen cannot be attacked by the f1-bishop since, if the knight jumps away from e2, then the d4-pawn will be lost.

12.♗d2 ♛c7 13.♗f4

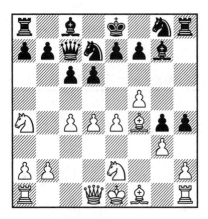

It would not be out of place here to spend a little time talking about the h4-g3 pawn standoff. In the great majority of such positions, it wouldn't be a good idea for White to take on h4, because then he'd be breaking up his pawn structure – which means that Black would not have to settle the position of his pawns right away.

One should maintain the tension for as long as possible, so as to operate with the threats of ...hxg3 or ...h4-h3. Let White keep thinking constantly about all these possibilities!

13...♞gf6

Black also has two other excellent possibilities in 13...b5 and 13...c5.

14.e5

A terrible blunder – which, it is true, goes unpunished.

14...♞h5

14...dxe5! 15.dxe5 ♞xe5! 16.♗g2 h3, and White is finished.

15.exd6 exd6 16.♕d2 ♘df6 17.0-0-0 ♗xf5 18.♘ac3 0-0-0 19.c5 ♘xf4 20.♕xf4 ♗h6

Once again, the white queen gets skewered. **0-1**

8. Jolki_palki (2056) – MASTER_GURU (2026)

11/02/2013

1.e4 d6 2.d4 h6 3.♘c3 c6 4.f4 g5 5.♘f3 ♗g7 6.f5

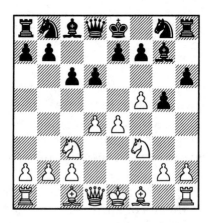

One more example of the theme of White's blocking the center with f4-f5.

6...♕a5

Not the best reaction. The typical ...g5-g4! is much stronger.

7.♗d3

It's still hard to be a trailblazer. This game was played in 2013, not long after I'd started to employ the Elshad System actively. Now, of course, I know that Black must play ...g5-g4! followed by just snapping off the d4-pawn, since the exchange of the d4-pawn for the g4-pawn isn't an even trade at all.

7...♘d7

7...g4! 8.♘d2 ♗xd4 9.♕xg4 h5! 10.♕e2 ♘d7 11.♘b3 ♗xc3+ 12.bxc3 ♕xc3+ 13.♗d2 ♕g7 14.0-0 h4:

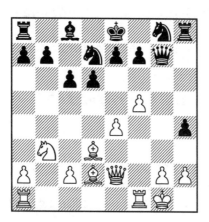

Black has both an extra pawn and an attack on White's king. He also has the center dark squares, especially e5. Because – just how powerful is a knight on e5, anyway?! Its power lies in the fact that no pawns can chase it away.

8.♗e3 ♘gf6!

Every time the bishop goes to e3, we bring our king's knight out to f6, threatening to leap to g4. But this position also holds another pair of interesting solutions with 8...c5 and 8...b5:

1) 8...c5!? 9.dxc5 ♗xc3+ 10.bxc3 ♕xc3+ 11.♗d2 ♕xc5∓. In view of the closed nature of the position, White's bishop pair isn't worth very much here.

2) 8...b5!? 9.0-0 ♘gf6 10.h3 g4 11.hxg4 ♘xg4 12.♗d2 ♕b6, with great play for Black.

9.0-0 ♞g4 10.♗d2 ♛b6 11.h3?

This is a mistake, but in any case the initiative (and a serious one) belongs to Black.

11...♗xd4+ 12.♞xd4 ♛xd4+ 13.♔h1 ♞f2+ 14.♖xf2 ♛xf2

In principle, this is the end. Continuing the game any further was unnecessary.

15.♗e1 ♛b6 16.♛d2 ♞e5 17.♗e2 ♗d7

17...♛xb2−+.

18.b3 g4 19.h4 g3 20.♞a4 ♛c7 21.♗xg3 0-0-0 22.♖d1 ♖dg8 23.♛e3 f6 24.♗f4 ♞g4 25.♗xg4 ♖xg4 26.g3 ♛a5 27.♞b2 d5 28.e5 c5 29.e6 ♗c6 30.♔h2 d4 31.♛e2 h5 32.♞d3 ♖hg8

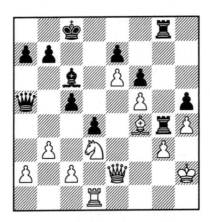

One feature of Elshad's System is that Black can mount an attack against White's king in the opening, in the middlegame, or even in the ending.

33.♞f2 ♖xf4 34.gxf4 ♖g2+ 35.♔h3 ♛d8

Look at how White might have been checkmated, and no less prettily (the variations are almost forcing!): 35...c4!! 36.bxc4 ♕xf5+ 37.♘g4 hxg4+ 38.♔xg4 ♕xg4#:

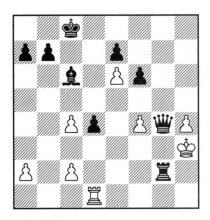

36.♕f1 ♕g8 37.♖d3 ♖g1

37...♕g4+! 38.♘xg4 hxg4#:

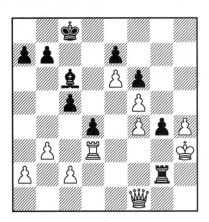

38.♕xg1 ♕xg1 39.♖g3 ♕xf2 40.♖g8+ ♔c7 41.♖g3 ♕f1+ 42.♔h2 ♕h1# 0-1

9. Ogayduk (2005) – MASTER-GURU (1845)

11/02/2013

1.d4 d6 2.c4 c6 3.♘c3 ♘d7 4.e4 h6 5.f4 g5 6.fxg5 ♗g7 7.gxh6 ♘xh6 8.♘f3 ♛b6

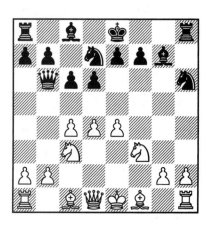

9.b3

In a standard position for this opening, White commits an error: he really has to shore up d4! Moreover, White has weakened his dark squares for no reason. The whole blame for this lies in knowing nothing about the upcoming positions. But how was White to know what needed to be done?

9...♘f8!

The knight follows the standard route d7-f8-e6, so as to attack the d4-pawn.

10.♗e3?!

A typical mistake by White. He has been visited by some illusion not only that his bishop will defend the d4-pawn, but also that White will, somewhere, sometime, be threatening to advance d4-d5, hitting the black queen.

10...♘g4! 11.♗g1 ♘e6

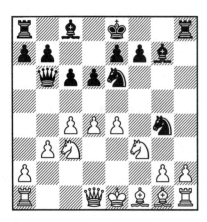

Let's look at the development of the pieces. Black is already clearly in the lead. It is difficult even to find some reasonable plan of action for White. The majority of those who encounter Elshad's System for the first time fall into this sort of situation.

12.♕d2 ♗h6 13.♕d3 ♕a5 14.h3 ♘f4 15.♕c2

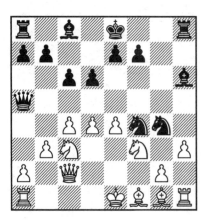

A critical moment in the opening. Here I made a typical move for this position, making use of the fact that White cannot take the g4-knight afterward. But it was also possible to simply retreat the knight to f6.

15...♗g7

15...♘f6!? would retain the bishop's station at h6, meaning that White wouldn't be able to castle long, owing to discovered check.

16.0-0-0 ♗e6

The immediate 16...c5! is better.

17.d5? ♗d7!

17...♗xc3 18.dxe6 ♘xe6 19.♗e2 ♘e5 20.♘xe5 ♗xe5 21.♗e3 ♕a3+ 22.♔b1 a5∓:

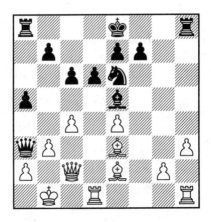

With a clear advantage for Black.

18.♘e2 ♘g6

The idea is well motivated, as the e5 square should be occupied, but it may be too early for the knight to leave its current position. An alternative would be 18...♕a3+!? 19.♔b1 ♘xe2 20.♗xe2 a5 21.♗d4 ♗xd4 22.♘xd4 ♘f2.

19.♗d4 ♘4e5

It is even better to trade bishops on d4. The dark squares around the white king would be weakened, while from d4 White's bishop can defend them: 19...♗xd4! 20.♘exd4, or 20.♖xd4 cxd5 21.exd5 ♘4e5

22.♘xe5 ♞xe5 23.♔b1 b5. This position is strongly reminiscent of the Dragon Variation, only it is Black alone who's attacking; White has no play whatever. Play might continue 20...♞e3 21.♕d2 ♕a3+ 22.♔b1 ♞xd1 23.♕xd1 c5 24.♘c2 ♕a5:

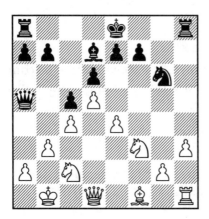

White has no real chances for salvation from this position.

20.♘xe5 ♗xe5 21.♗xe5 ♞xe5 22.♘d4

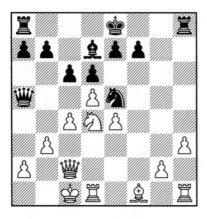

22...c5

An inaccuracy, apparently. Here Black has to open up the game against White's king. That being necessary, 22...cxd5!? 23.exd5 ♖c8 24.♔b1 b5 should be considered.

23.♘f5 ♗xf5

As a rule, in this opening, this move must be made almost without thinking. Look at the pieces that *remain* on the board. Compare the knight on e5 with White's bishop.

24.exf5 ♔d7!

A very strong move. The rooks have to be connected, but along with that, the queen's rook should remain in place in order to attack the white king.

25.♗e2 f6 26.g4

White's last chance. Certainly he understands that, soon, an assault will fall upon his king on a grand scale; so he drives his own pawns forward.

26...a6 27.h4 b5 28.g5 bxc4!

We have to open lines.

29.♗xc4 ♖ab8 30.g6 ♖b4 31.h5 ♖hb8 32.h6

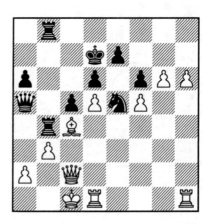

A picturesque position. White is on the verge of promoting his pawns, but he gets mated instead!

32...♛a3+?

32...♜xc4–+ wins outright after 33.bxc4 ♛a3+ 34.♔d2 ♜b2.

33.♔d2??

Mutual mistakes in chess – a frequent occurrence. As Savielly Tartakower once said, what matters is who makes the final mistake.

33.♛b2 ♛xb2+ 34.♔xb2 ♞xc4+ 35.♔a1 ♞e3 36.h7 ♞xf5 37.g7 ♞xg7 38.♜dg1 ♜h8 39.♜xg7 ♜bb8 40.♜e1 ♜be8 41.♔b2±.

33...♜xc4 34.bxc4 ♜b2 35.♜c1 ♛d3+ 36.♔e1 ♜xc2 37.♜xc2 ♛xc2 38.g7 ♞d3+ 39.♔f1 ♛f2# 0-1

10. Feodal (2679) – Nemtsev_Igor (2835)

2/27/2015

1.d4 c6 2.c4 d6 3.♞c3 ♞d7 4.e4 h6 5.f4 g5 6.♞f3 ♝g7 7.fxg5 ♞f8 8.♝e2

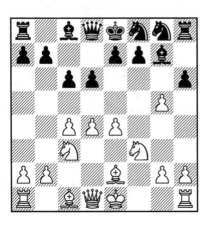

Kind of a half-measure. Taking on h6 looks risky for White.

8...♞e6

But the current state of "theory" on the Elshad System states that here is where you *have* to take on g5! The point is that, after my ...♘e6, then g5-g6 becomes possible. In that event, the game takes a completely different path.

9.gxh6

9.g6!? fxg6 10.♕d3 ♘f8 11.♗d2 favors White.

9...♘xh6 10.0-0 ♕b6 11.♗e3?

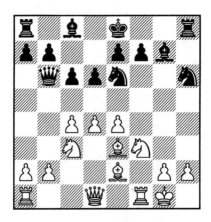

There already were three pieces attacking the d4-pawn. 11.♘a4! (that's how White needs to continue) 11...♕a5 12.♗d2 ♕c7 13.d5 ♘d4 14.♘xd4 ♗xd4+ 15.♔h1 ♗e5, and the whole struggle still lies ahead. The computer continually shows an advantage for White, but he still must be smart enough to play the position.

11...♕xb2

Not the best choice. The routine 11...♘g4! ensures Black the advantage: 12.♗f2 ♘xf2 13.♖xf2 ♘xd4.

12.♖c1

12.♘a4 ♕a3 13.♗c1 ♕b4 14.a3 ♕a5 15.h3 ♗d7.

12...♘g4

Black doesn't need to be asked twice.

13.♖c2 ♛b6 14.c5 ♛c7?

14...dxc5–+ (we already know that such pawns must be wiped out at once) 15.dxc5 ♛c7. White's e3-bishop hangs, plus mate is threatened on h2. White's position is hopeless.

15.cxd6 ♛xd6

Black has not totally thrown away his advantage. He must bear down once more.

16.e5 ♛b4

16...♘xe3!? 17.exd6 ♘xd1 18.♖xd1 exd6 19.g3 d5∓ seems simpler: the evaluation would be pretty clear.

17.♗d2 ♘xd4 18.♘e4

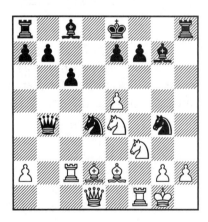

18...♘xe2+

This doesn't let the win slip away, but ...♘xf3+ is simpler. White's knight is exactly the piece Black needs to get rid of. The knight is the defender, not only of the king, but also of the squares h2 and d4: 18...♘xf3+! 19.♗xf3 ♛d4+ 20.♘f2 ♗xe5 21.h3 ♘xf2 22.♖xf2 ♗g3 23.♛e1 ♛xf2+ 24.♛xf2 ♗xf2+ 25.♔xf2 ♗f5−+.

19.♛xe2 ♛b6+ 20.♔h1 ♗xe5

20...♗f5 21.♖c4 0-0-0.

21.h3 ♗e6 22.♘xe5 ♘xe5 23.♘c5

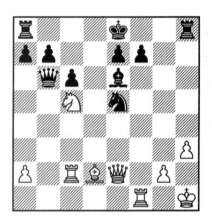

23...♗xh3

This bishop sacrifice is not correct. But I suggest that you watch to the end, to see how it's still so difficult to fight when your king's situation is bad, even up a rook. In the end, White couldn't stand the tension and lost.

23...♛b5 leaves Black with a small plus.

24.gxh3 ♖xh3+ 25.♔g2 0-0-0 26.♔xh3 f6 27.♗f4 ♖h8+ 28.♔g3 ♖g8+ 29.♔f2 ♘g4+ 30.♔f3 e5 31.♖g1 f5 32.♗xe5 ♛b4 33.♛c4 ♘xe5+ 34.♔e2 ♘xc4 35.♖xg8+ ♔c7 36.♖g7+ ♔d6 37.♘xb7+ ♔e5 38.♖e7+ ♔f6 39.♖c7 ♘e5 40.♖7xc6+ ♘xc6 41.♖xc6+ ♔g5 42.♘d6 ♛a4 43.♖c3 f4 44.♔d3 ♛a6+ 45.♘c4 ♛d6+ 46.♔c2 ♛f6 47.♖d3 f3 48.♖d5+ ♔g4 49.♘e3+ ♔h3 50.♘f5 ♛xf5+ 51.♖d3 ♔g3 52.♔c3 ♛f4 53.♖xf3+ ♛xf3+ 0-1

11. FVV (2619) – Nemtsev_Igor (2617)

4/19/2015

1.c4 c6 2.♘c3 d6 3.d4 ♘d7 4.e4 h6 5.f4 g5 6.fxg5 ♗g7 7.gxh6 ♘xh6 8.♗e2

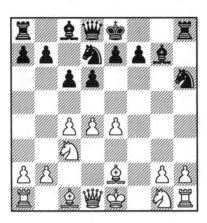

White's problem is that he just can't do without developing his king's knight.

8...♛b6

This is the main move, but there's also another good possibility – namely, 8...c5!?. After this, White can defend d4 in two different ways, with ♘f3 or ♗e3. In addition, he can advance to d5 or trade on c5. Let's examine each of these ideas in turn:

1) 9.♘f3 cxd4 10.♘xd4, and here Black has a couple of moves promising terrific play on the dark squares: 10...♛b6 or 10...♗e5.

2) 9.♗e3 cxd4 10.♗xd4 ♗xd4 11.♛xd4 ♖g8. White will find it very hard to come up with something. Black has excellent support points on e5 and c5. Meanwhile, White's exact plan is still nebulous.

3) 9.d5 ♘e5 10.♘f3 ♘hg4 11.♘xe5 ♘xe5. Castling kingside looks rather scary for White here; Black has comfortable play on the dark squares.

Chapter 1

4) 9.dxc5 ♘xc5 10.♘f3 ♘g4 11.0-0 ♗xc3 12.bxc3 ♕b6 13.♔h1 ♘xe4 14.♕d4 ♘g3+ 15.♔g1 ♘xe2+ 16.♔h1 ♘xd4−+. This variation illustrates the power of Black's attack.

9.♘f3 ♘f8 10.♘a4 ♕a5+ 11.♗d2

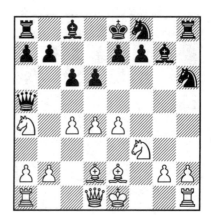

11...♕c7

In addition to the text, Black also has the classic queen transfer to the kingside with 11...♕h5! 12.0-0 ♕g6 13.♘c3 ♖g8 14.g3 (the threat was 14...♗xd4) 14...♘g4 15.♔g2 ♗xd4 16.♘xd4 ♘xh2 17.♗e1 ♘xf1 18.♗xf1 ♕h7, reorganizing for an attack down the h-file. Black's advantage is clear.

12.♘c3 ♘e6 13.♗e3 ♘g4 14.♗g1 ♕a5 15.♕d2 ♗h6 16.♕c2 ♘e3 17.♕a4?

After this move, the game should have ended quickly, since Black could simply win the rook.

An important lesson I learned from studying this opening is that you have to constantly examine queen trades. It looks like you don't need to trade them if you can maintain a strong attack with them on the board; but in fact, more often than not a queen trade is necessary. And the force of the attack, as a rule, is not dissipated by that exchange.

17...♘xg2+

17...♕xa4! 18.♘xa4 ♘c2+ 19.♔d1 ♘xa1–+.

18.♔f2 ♕h5 19.♔xg2 ♘f4+ 20.♔f2

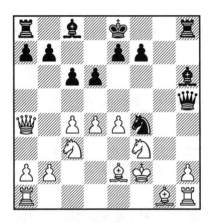

Of course, the white king is in great danger. But we need to find the strongest moves.

20...♗g4

20...♖g8 is very strong – adding the rook to the attack decides. 21.♗f1 ♘h3+ 22.♗xh3 ♗xh3 23.♘e2 ♖g2+ 24.♔e1 ♕xf3 25.♕d1 ♕xe4. White can't last more than seven moves, at most. Mate is unavoidable.

21.♕d1 ♖g8 22.h3 0-0-0 23.hxg4 ♕xh1 24.g5 ♘h3+ 25.♔e3 ♘xg5 26.♘xg5 ♖xg5 27.♔d3 d5 28.cxd5 cxd5 29.♘xd5 ♖dxd5 30.♖c1+ ♔b8 31.exd5

A highly unusual attack. It seems as though White's king has fought its way out of the danger zone, but now 31...♖g3+ would have ended things.

31...♕xd5

31...♖g3+ 32.♔c2 ♗xc1 33.♕xc1 ♕e4+ 34.♔d2 ♕f4+ 35.♔c2 ♕f5+ 36.♔d2 ♕g5+ 37.♔c2 ♕g6+ 38.♔d2 ♖g1–+.

32.♗h2+ e5 33.♔c2 ♖g2 34.♗xe5+ ♔a8 35.♔b1 ♗xc1 36.♗f3 ♖xb2+ 37.♔xc1 ♕xa2 38.♗xb7+ ♖xb7 39.♕c2 ♕xc2+ 40.♔xc2 ♖d7

White hasn't been mated (yet), but the endgame is completely hopeless. **0-1**

12. Vgl_power (2790) – Nemtsev_Igor (2709)

4/18/2015

1.d4 c6 2.c4 d6 3.♘c3 ♘d7 4.e4 h6 5.f4 g5 6.fxg5 ♗g7 7.gxh6 ♘xh6 8.♘f3 ♘f8 9.♗d3?!

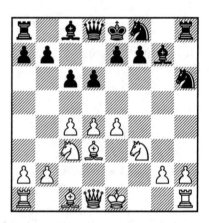

This whole variation is not good for White. And if you need a concrete reason, then: moving ♗f1-d3 allows Black to exert pressure on the d4-pawn freely, since on d3 the bishop interferes with the pawn's natural defense by the queen.

9...♘e6! 10.d5?!

The most natural reaction to the attack on the d4-pawn, but also a mistake. White has other possibilities:

1) 10.♗c2!? ♘g4!? 11.h3 ♕b6 12.♘e2 ♕b4+ (12...c5!? 13.d5 ♘f8) 13.♗d2 ♕xc4 and, despite what the engine says about who is better, it's a lot easier to play Black here. White is defending desperately after just ten moves, and that of course is not a healthy situation to be in;

2) 10.♘e2 ♕a5+ 11.♗d2 ♕b6 12.♗c3 c5 13.d5 ♘d4 14.♘exd4 cxd4 15.♗d2 ♘g4, and Black totally has the initiative.

10...♘c5 11.♗e3?!

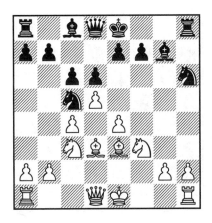

11...♘xd3+

Here Black had the outstanding possibility 11...♕b6!. Since the bishop has been developed to e3, now the b2-pawn is weakened! In addition, the a1-h8 diagonal comes open.

Let's see: 12.♗xc5 (12.♖b1 ♘g4 13.♗g1 ♕a5 14.♕d2 ♗xc3 15.bxc3 ♘xd3+ 16.♕xd3 ♕xa2∓; 12.♕c2?? ♕xb2 13.♕xb2 ♘xd3+ 14.♔e2 ♘xb2−+) 12...♕xb2! 13.0-0 (13.♗d4 ♗xd4 14.♘xd4 ♕xc3+ 15.♔f1 ♕xd4 is totally hopeless for White) 13...dxc5 14.♘e2 ♘g4 15.♖b1 ♕f6 16.♕d2 ♗h6 17.♕b2 ♗e3+ 18.♔h1 ♖xh2+ 19.♘xh2 ♕h6, and mate cannot be avoided.

12.♕xd3 c5

In most cases, I play just like this. But the author of the system, Elshad, likes other moves:

1) 12...♘g4!? 13.♗d4 ♗xd4 14.♕xd4 f6 15.h3 ♖h5 16.0-0-0 ♘e5 17.♘xe5 ♖xe5 with a very non-standard game;

2) 12...♕a5 13.0-0 ♘g4 14.♗d2 *[14.♗d4 – Ed.]* 14...♕b6+ 15.♔h1 ♘f2+ 16.♖xf2 ♕xf2 17.♖f1 ♕g3 18.♕e2 ♗g4 19.♕f2 ♕xf2 20.♖xf2 ♖c8.

13.0-0-0 ♘g4 14.♗g1 ♕a5

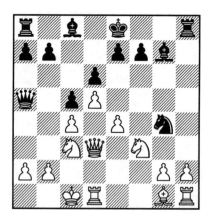

Starting an immediate attack on the white king. As usual in this opening, it is Black who attacks, while White doesn't even have a target for his own attack – just "aahs" and "ohhs." How is it that Black can violate the basic principles of the opening? Black still has his king in the center.

15.♔b1 a6

Slowing the tempo of the attack a bit. There are other promising moves:

1) 15...♗d7!? 16.♖c1 b5 17.♘xb5 ♗xb5 18.cxb5 a6 19.bxa6 ♖xa6 20.a3 0-0!! 21.h3 ♖b8 22.♖c2 ♘e5 23.♘xe5 ♗xe5 24.♗e3 ♖ab6, and White has no defense;

2) 15...♗xc3!? 16.♕xc3 ♕xc3 17.bxc3 ♘f6 18.♖e1 ♘xe4 19.♔b2 (19.♖xe4 ♗f5) 19...♗f5.

16.h3 b5

Let us not forget that the g4-knight is not hanging, so we can quietly keep attacking.

17.cxb5 ♘e5

The more standard 17...axb5 is also interesting: 18.♕xb5+ ♕xb5 19.♘xb5 ♖a4 20.♘c3 ♗xc3 21.bxc3 ♘f6 22.e5 ♗f5+ 23.♔b2 ♘e4 24.exd6 0-0 25.dxe7 ♖b8+ 26.♔c1 ♖xa2 27.e8♕+ ♖xe8. Then the rook comes back and there is no salvation for White.

18.♘xe5 ♗xe5 19.b6 ♕xb6 20.♗e3 ♖b8 21.♕c2 ♕b4

Such a position cannot be defended, by any human standard.

22.♗d2 ♗d7 23.a3?

Of course this is a blunder, but Black has an overwhelming attack in any case.

23...♕xa3 24.♖hf1 ♖b3 25.♔c1 ♕a1+ 26.♕b1 ♕a5 27.♔c2 ♗a4 28.♘a4 ♕a4 29.♔c1 ♔d7!!

The h8-rook joins Black's offensive to decisive effect.

30.♖f3 ♖hb8 31.♖b3 ♖xb3 32.♗c3 ♗xc3 33.bxc3 ♖xb1+ 0-1

13. Vgl_power (2780) – Nemtsev_Igor (2719)

4/18/2015

1.d4 c6 2.c4 d6 3.♘c3 ♘d7 4.e4 h6 5.f4 g5 6.fxg5 ♗g7 7.gxh6 ♘xh6 8.♘f3 ♘f8 9.♗d3 ♘e6 10.d5 ♘c5 11.♗e3 ♕b6!

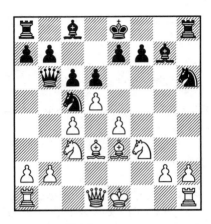

This is how the theory of the Elshad System develops: my opponent makes a second attempt to rehabilitate his variation, which I ride out to meet, fully armed.

12.♘a4

And right away comes the decisive mistake.

12...♛b4+ 13.♗d2

13.♘c3 ♛xb2! winning a whole piece, at least.

13...♛xa4 14.♗c2 ♛xc4

As they say, White did not even make it out of the opening.

14. Kosmosss (2203) – NemtsevIgor (2213)

Live Chess on Chess.com 6/11/2015

1.d4 c6 2.c4 d6 3.e4 h6 4.♘c3 ♘d7 5.f4 g5 6.fxg5 ♗g7 7.♘f3 hxg5 8.♗xg5 ♛b6 9.♛d2 ♘f8 10.♗e3

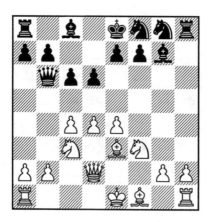

10...♘f6!?

Despite Black's quick (and spectacular) victory, this move cannot really be viewed as best. The thing is that, in this position – and, in fact, in the entire Elshad System – it is important to control the e5 square (10...♘h6!).

11.d5 c5 12.♗d3?!

Here White could have played the break e4-e5!, which became possible when Black failed to play ...♘g8-h6. For example, 12.e5!? dxe5 (12...♘g4 13.exd6 ♘xe3 14.♕xe3 ♕xd6 15.♘b5 ♕d8 16.♕xc5±) 13.♘xe5 ♘h5 14.♘d3 ♘g3 15.♖g1 ♖xh2 16.♗f4 ♗h6 17.0-0-0 ♗xf4 18.♕xf4 ♕h6 19.♕xh6 ♖xh6 20.♘xc5. One should acknowledge that White has a small but stable advantage here.

12...♘g4 13.♗g1 ♗h6 14.♕e2 ♘g6 15.g3??

The fatal mistake. White didn't want to let Black's knight to land on f4.

15...♘6e5?!

It's better to send the other knight to e5 (15...♘4e5!), as then Black would have the pinning threat ...♗g4.

16.♘xe5 ♘xe5

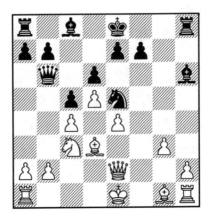

White resigned. He has no reasonable move (17.h3 ♕xb2; 17.♖b1 ♗g4 18.♕c2 ♗f3). As an aside, this position belongs to the "theory" of the Elshad System: I knew it, and my opponent didn't.

0-1

15. Azizian – Elshad

2007

1.c4 c6 2.d4 d6 3.e4 ♘d7 4.♘c3 h6 5.f4 g5 6.fxg5 hxg5 7.♗xg5 ♕b6 8.♕d2 ♘h6

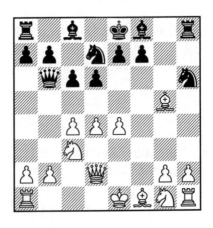

Instead of the standard ...♗g7; the difference is insignificant. If White castles long, then Black wins a tempo – incidentally getting his bishop to h6 in a single move. So how does White play now?

9.♘f3

9.♗e2!? temporarily prevents Black's knight from reaching g4. 9...♗g7 10.♘f3 ♘f8 transposes to "normal/theoretical" lines for this opening.

9...♘g4 10.♗d3

10.h3 – this move we will ignore, as usual, since it doesn't actually threaten the knight on g4 as White would lose the h1-rook: 10... f6 11.♗f4 ♕a5 12.0-0-0 e5 13.♗g3?? ♗h6–+.

10...♗g7

10...f6 11.h3 fxg5 12.0-0-0 ♘gf6 13.e5.

11.♗c2

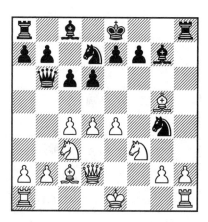

11...♘f8

In this concrete situation, 11...♕xb2 is not very good, since it gives White time to hide his king away: 12.0-0 ♕b6 13.♖ab1 ♕c7 14.h3 ♘h6, and the first of the attacking waves has been beaten back.

The best move is 11...f6!. The idea is to drive White's dark-squared bishop away, and ideally off the c1-h6 diagonal. In that event, our own dark-squared bishop would go to h6, followed by a decisive invasion on the dark squares. Now:

1) 12.♗f4 e5 13.♗g3 ♗h6 14.♕d3 exd4 15.♕xd4 ♕xb2 (this is the time!) 16.♘d1 ♕xc2–+;

2) 12.c5 dxc5 13.♘a4 ♕d8 14.♗e3 ♘xe3 15.♕xe3 ♕a5+ 16.♕c3 ♕c3+ 17.bxc3 cxd4 18.cxd4 b5 19.♘c3 ♗h6, with a complex ending where Black enjoys the better chances.

12.♖b1?

And now White's king is definitively stranded in the center. The weakness of the king in this situation is determined by the fact that it's defended only by other pieces. Around the white king there lies emptiness – see especially the dark squares.

On the other hand, after 12.0-0-0!? ♘e6 13.h3 ♘xg5 14.♘xg5 ♘h6 15.e5!± the battle is far from over.

12...♘e6

13.♗e3

13.♗h4 ♘xd4 14.♘xd4 ♖xh4 15.♘f3 ♖h5 16.h3 ♗e6 17.♗d3 0-0-0!–+; or 13.♘a4!? (the best of a bad lot; the point is to drive the black queen away from the d4-pawn) 13...♕c7 14.♗e3 ♘xe3 15.♕xe3 ♗h6 16.♕f2 ♘f4 17.♘c3 ♖g8, and Black is clearly on top.

13...♕a5

13...♘xe3! 14.♕xe3 ♘xd4 15.♘xd4 ♗xd4 16.♕d2 ♗e5, and White's position is hopeless.

14.♗g1 ♗h6 15.♕d1 ♘f4∓ 16.♔f1 ♕h5 17.♘e2

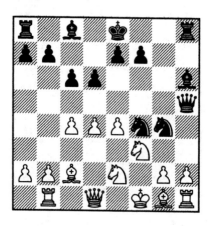

17...♘e3+!

A typical shot: 17...♘xg2!? 18.♔xg2 ♘e3+ 19.♗xe3 ♗xe3 20.h4 ♖g8+ 21.♘g5 ♗g4! 22.♗d3 ♗f3+ 23.♔h2 ♕xh4+ 24.♘h3 ♖g2#:

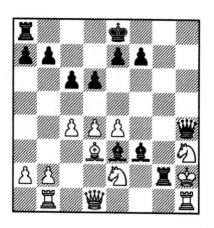

18.♗xe3 ♘xg2 19.♔xg2

19.♗xh6 ♕xf3+ 20.♔g1 ♘e3 21.♗xe3 ♗h3 22.♕f1 ♗xf1 23.♖xf1 ♖g8+ 24.♗g5 ♖xg5+ 25.♘g3 ♖xg3+ 26.hxg3 ♕xg3#.

19...♗xe3 20.h4

Not 20.♘g3 ♗h3#.

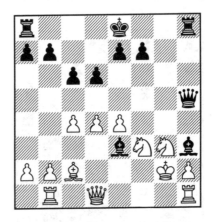

20...♖g8+ 21.♘g3 ♖xg3+ 22.♔xg3 ♕g4+ 23.♔h2 ♕h3#.
0-1

16. Shchukin Dm. – Elshad

5/20/2015

Dmitry Shchukin is a decent player, a strong candidate master *[equivalent to USCF National Master – Ed.]* whom both Elshad and I know well. A distinguishing feature of his playing style is his unrealistic clinging to principles. He goes in for all the main lines, munching on every pawn and piece that you offer him. With players of this kind, one must absolutely play Elshad's System (even if you're not going in for the best lines), independently of whether he plays c2-c4.

1.d4 d6 2.e4

Just so! White does have the opportunity to play this. It's all well and good. All the more interesting to see how the system's inventor brings his ideas to life!

2...♘d7 3.♘c3 h6 4.f4 g5

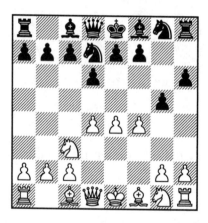

Following our scheme! The difference from the positions where White plays c2-c4 is that, in the first place, White has the possibility in some lines to shore up the d4-pawn with c2-c3; and, secondly, that White's f1-bishop might come out to c4, which of course holds out improved prospects for White.

5.fxg5

5.e5!? would disrupt Black's plans, unfortunately. Of course, the battle is far from over. But White still has the advantage here. Well, OK! So let White analyze this himself! But I won't be helping him.

5...hxg5 6.♗xg5

As I told you, Dmitry takes everything – always!

6...c6

Opening a path for the queen.

7.♕d2 ♖h5

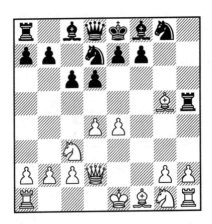

Now, where, in what other opening, would you see that?!

8.♗e3

8.♗e2!? is relatively best: 8...♖xg5 9.♕xg5 ♕b6! 10.♖b1 (10.0-0-0 ♗h6−+; 10.♕xg8 ♕xb2 11.♖d1 ♕xc3+ 12.♔f1 ♕xc2∓) 10...♘gf6 11.e5 dxe5 12.dxe5 ♕a5 13.♘f3 ♘e4 14.♕e3 ♘xc3 15.♕xc3 ♕xc3+ 16.bxc3 ♗g7 17.0-0 ♘xe5 18.♘xe5 ♗xe5 19.c4 b6 20.g4 ♗e6 21.h4 f6 22.♔g2 ♔f7, with counterplay. This line is not absolutely forced, but it does illustrate both sides' possibilities.

8...♘gf6 9.0-0-0 ♖a5!!

Very original – and consistent, too!

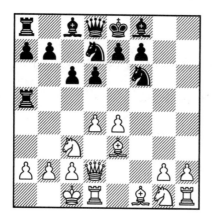

10.♘f3 b5

That a5-rook is simply mesmerizing Dmitry. He wants to capture it so much that, ironically, he ends up making a computer move, b2-b4. Although *Houdini* totally agrees with this, look at the difference in the way a human plays it.

11.b4 ♖a3 12.♔b2

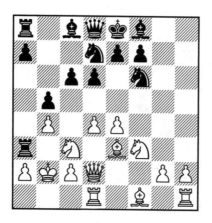

12...a5!!

Houdini found this too, and after five minutes' thinking said that the position now favors Black!

13.♔xa3

Now this is forced, as otherwise, Black is attacking for free.

13...axb4+ 14.♔b2

14.♔xb4 ♛a5+ 15.♔b3 ♛a3#.

14...♛a5 15.a4?

It's easy to lose your way in this sort of situation. He has to drop the knight back to b1.

15.♘b1 (forced) 15...♘xe4 16.♛e1 ♘c3 17.♔c1 (17.♘xc3?? ♛a3+ 18.♔b1 bxc3) 17...♘xb1 18.♔xb1 ♘f6! (new soldiers take the place of the fallen!) 19.♔c1 ♗f5 20.♗d3 ♛a3+ 21.♔d2 ♗xd3 22.cxd3 ♛b2#.

15...♘b6 16.♘b1

16.♖a1 (the final defensive barricade) 16...bxc3+ 17.♛xc3 ♘xa4+ 18.♖xa4 ♛xa4 19.♗d3 ♗e6 20.d5 ♘xd5 21.exd5 ♗xd5 22.♖e1 ♗xf3 23.gxf3 ♗g7 24.♛xg7 ♛b4+ 25.♔c1 ♛xe1+ 26.♔b2 ♛a1+ 27.♔b3 ♛a3#.

16...♘xe4 17.♛d3 ♘xa4+

The mate with two knights which the reader will shortly see, is so pretty that I have never before witnessed such a beautiful conclusion!

18.♔c1 ♘ac3 19.♘fd2 ♗f5 20.♖e1 ♕a1 21.♗f4 ♘f2 22.♕xf5 ♘a2#

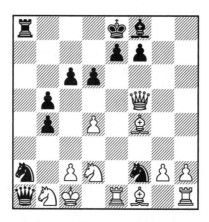

And you, dear reader – have you ever seen anything like that? Ever played a mate like this? **0-1**

17. Sandro_Mikanovic (2197) – Nemtsev_Igor (2283)

Live Chess on Chess.com 7/12/2015

1.d4 c6 2.c4 d6 3.♘c3 ♘d7 4.e4 h6 5.f4 g5 6.fxg5 hxg5 7.♗xg5 ♗g7 8.♘f3 ♘f8 9.♕d2 ♘e6 10.♗e3 ♘h6 11.d5

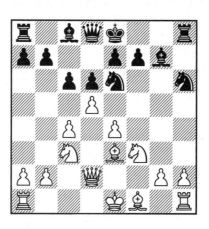

This position comes up so often that we might call it a *tabiya* of the Elshad. As we have said before, the d4-d5 advance is more likely to favor Black, because the newly opened diagonal will belong to him. And – what is most important – now the e5 square has passed completely into Black's hands!

11...♘f8

"The Moor has done his duty; the Moor can go" (Schiller). In other words, the knight put pressure on the d4-pawn, induced it to move forward, and now can go back to f8 – so as to go forward again along a different route, f8-g6-e5!

12.♗d4

I played a fascinating seven-game match against Sandro Mikanović, a master from Bosnia-Herzegovina. The score was 6-1 in favor of our opening!

12...♗xd4 13.♕xd4 f6!

This is a standard device in this pawn structure. It is often encountered in the Sicilian Dragon. The pawns on f6 and d6 remind me of a pair of horns that inhibit the e4-pawn from advancing to e5.

14.0-0-0 c5 15.♕d2 ♘g4 16.h3 ♕a5

Here it would have been better to play my knight to g6 *en route* to e5: 16...♘g6! 17.♖e1 ♘4e5 18.♗e2 a6 19.♘xe5 ♘xe5 20.♘d1 b5 21.♔b1 ♕b6. Black is attacking; and what is White doing?

17.♗d3 ♘e5 18.♘xe5 fxe5

18...dxe5!?.

19.♔b1 a6 20.♘e2

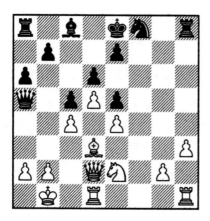

20...♕c7

20...♕xd2 21.♖xd2 ♘g6 22.♗c2 ♗g4 23.♘c3 ♘f4 24.♖f1 ♗d7. Chances in this ending are equal: White's extra pawn is very hard to advance. White's bishop can be numbered among the bad ones, while all of Black's pieces are very active.

21.g4 ♗d7 22.♔a1 b5 23.b3 ♕b6 24.♖dg1

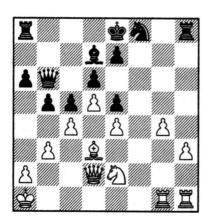

24...a5!

In this kind of position it is necessary to open lines as much as possible, especially near the opposing king.

25.cxb5 ♗xb5 26.a4 ♗xd3 27.♕xd3 ♖b8 28.♔a2

28.♕b5+ ♕xb5 29.axb5 ♖xb5 30.♔a2 ♘g6 31.♖f1 ♖b4 32.♘g3 ♘f4 33.h4 0-0!. How do you like that – castling (and on move 33!), leading to a winning endgame!

28...♘g6 29.g5 ♕b4 30.♖g4

30...0-0!!

30...♖f8 31.♖h2 ♖f1 32.♕c3 ♕b6 (32...♖a1+!! 33.♔xa1 *[33.♕xa1 ♕xb3#]* 33...♕a3+ 34.♔b1 ♖xb3+ 35.♕xb3 ♕xb3+ 36.♔c1 ♕a3+ 37.♔d2 c4 38.♖g3 ♕b2+ 39.♔d1 ♕b1+ 40.♔d2 ♕xe4-+) 33.h4 ♔d7 34.h5 ♘f4 35.♘xf4 exf4 36.h6 c4 37.♕xc4 ♖f2+ 38.♖xf2 ♕xf2+ 39.♔a3 ♕f3 40.h7 ♕h3 41.g6 ♕h1 42.♕c6+ ♔d8 43.♖g1 ♕h3 44.♕c4 ♖c8 45.g7 ♖xc4 46.g8♕+ ♔c7 47.♕f8 ♖xa4+.

31.♖h2 c4 32.♕xc4 ♕d2+ 33.♔a3 ♖bc8 34.♕b5 ♖c2 35.b4 ♖a2+ 36.♔b3 ♕c2#

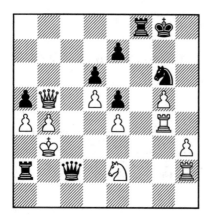

0-1

18. Sandro_Mikanovic (2185) – Nemtsev_Igor (2295)

Live Chess on Chess.com 7/12/2015

1.d4 c6 2.e4 d6 3.f4 ♘d7 4.♘f3 h6 5.♗d3 g5

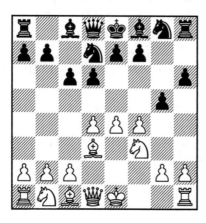

Black chooses a line known to be risky. The problem is that, since White has not yet pushed his c2-pawn to c4, he can still play it to c3, shoring up his d4-pawn.

6.fxg5 ♗g7 7.gxh6 ♘xh6 8.c3 c5

There is no other way to undermine the d4-pawn.

9.d5?!

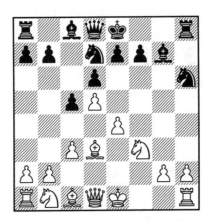

This impulsive thrust weakens the a7-g1 diagonal.

9...♘g4 10.♘bd2 c4!?

10...♘de5!? 11.♘xe5 ♘xe5 12.♗e2 ♕c7 13.0-0 c4.

11.♗e2?

A terrible blunder, which I failed to exploit, even though I had seen the ...♘e3 riposte.

11...♕b6

11...♘e3!–+ 12.♕a4 0-0! 13.♘xc4 ♘c5 14.♕b5 ♗d7, and the queen is trapped.

12.♖f1 ♘e3 13.♘xc4 ♘xg2+ 14.♔d2 ♕c7 15.♔c2

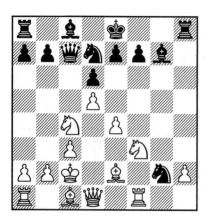

15...b5

The hunt for the white king continues. When he sat down to play this game, White could hardly have wanted to reach this position.

16.♘e3 ♘f4 17.♗xb5 ♖b8 18.♗a4?

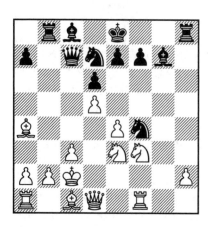

A mistake; now Black can get at White's king.

18.♗c6!? ♗a6 19.c4 ♕b6 20.♘f5 ♗xc4 21.♘xg7+ ♔d8 22.b3 ♗d3+ 23.♔b2 ♖h2+ 24.♘h2 ♕d4+ 25.♔a3 ♘e5 26.♗d2 ♘c4+ 27.bxc4

♕b2+ 28.♔a4 ♗c2+ 29.♕xc2 ♕xc2+ 30.♔a3 ♕xd2 and, although this is not absolutely forced, it's still pretty spectacular. I present it as an example of the strength of Black's attack.

18...♗a6 19.♘d4 ♗d3+ 20.♔d2 ♖xh2+ 21.♔e1 ♗xd4 22.♖xf4

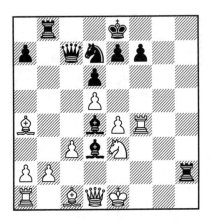

22...♖e2+

Black wins much more quickly with 22...♗xe3: 23.♗xe3 ♖h1+ 24.♔d2 ♖xd1+ 25.♖xd1 ♗b5 26.♗xb5 ♖xb5; or 23.♕xd3 ♗xf4 24.♗xf4 ♖h1+ 25.♔f2 ♖xb2+ 26.♔g3 ♖xa1 27.♗c6 ♖g1+ 28.♔f3 ♔d8 29.♕e3 ♖f1+ 30.♔g3 ♘f6, and any commentary would be superfluous.

23.♕xe2 ♗xe2 24.♔xe2 ♗f6 25.♗c6 ♖b6 26.♗d2 ♖xc6!

Correct! Here the queen will prove much stronger than the white rooks, for the simple reason that White's king is exposed and will fall constantly under a variety of tactical threats.

27.dxc6 ♕xc6 28.♘d5 ♘e5?!

28...♗g5–+ 29.♖g4 ♕b5+ 30.♔d1 ♕xb2 31.♖c1 ♕xd2#.

29.♘xf6+ exf6 30.♖af1

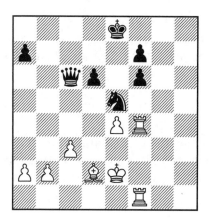

So many mistakes – and yet, Black is still winning. Now the main factor is the queen-and-knight super-combination. All in all, ♕+♘ is the strongest attacking pair against the king.

30...♕b5+ 31.♔d1 ♕xb2 32.♖xf6 ♘c4 33.♖1f2 ♕b1+ 34.♔e2 ♕xe4+ 35.♔f1 ♕d3+ 36.♖e2+ ♔f8 37.♖ff2 ♘xd2+ 38.♔e1 ♘e4 0-1

19. ecutelem (1951) – NemtsevIgor (2088)

Live Chess on Chess.com 5/9/2015

1.e4 c6 2.f4

From the standpoint of Elshad's System, this is already a mistake. Since Black has already provoked White into playing f2-f4, he can later attack the pawn with ...g7-g5. The dark squares are thus weakened, particularly around White's king.

2...d6

For those who play the Caro-Kann, I remind you that here the best choice (rather than 2...d6) is 2...d5!, transposing into a form of the Caro-Kann that is very favorable to Black.

3.♘f3 h6 4.d3

But this looks strange. Why not 4.d4 ?

4...g5

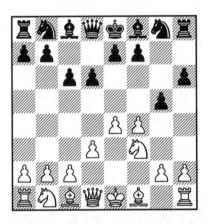

You'll agree that White would never expect this move. After all, g5 is attacked three times!

5.♗e2 ♗g7 6.fxg5 ♘d7 7.gxh6 ♘xh6 8.0-0

(see diagram next page)

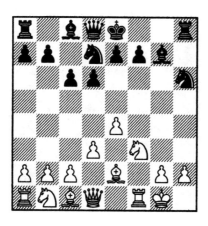

8...♞g4

The standard move in these kinds of positions. Yet this particular position contains certain subtleties that lead to other ideas:

1) 8...♞e5 9.d4 ♞xf3+ 10.♗xf3 ♛b6 11.c3 c5 12.d5 ♗e5 13.h3 c4+ 14.♔h1 ♞g8 15.♛e2 ♗xh3 16.gxh3 ♜xh3+ 17.♔g2 ♜h2#:

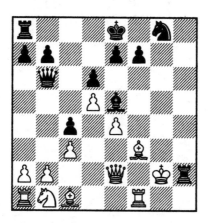

2) 8...d5 9.exd5 ♛c7! (focusing on the h2-square) 10.dxc6 ♞g4 11.cxd7+ ♗xd7 12.h3 ♗d4+ 13.♔h1 (13.♞xd4 ♛h2#) 13...♗c6 14.♞c3 ♜xh3+ 15.gxh3 ♛h2#:

A very pretty mate!

3) 8...f5 9.exf5 ♘xf5 10.d4 ♛b6 11.c3 e5.

9.h3 ♛b6+ 10.d4 ♘de5

This move involves sacrificing material. It is also possible to attack "without paying for it": 10...♘ge5! 11.c3 ♘xf3+ 12.♗xf3 c5 13.d5 ♘e5 14.♛e2 ♖g8 15.♔h1 ♗d7 16.♘d2 ♗b5 17.c4 ♗d7 18.♖b1 0-0-0 19.b4 ♖h8 20.bxc5 ♛xc5.

11.hxg4

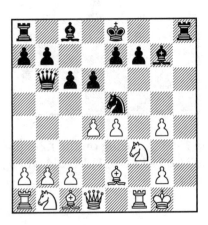

It would not be out of order to point out that in chess, along with the "objective" evaluation of the position, there is also the psychological angle. In chess, we play against human beings. Experience teaches us that fighting our way out of such positions while holding on to our extra material, is something that only a very few can do. And it is especially difficult to defend as White when you're playing rapid or blitz chess.

11...♘xg4

11...♘xf3+ 12.gxf3 (on 12.♗xf3, 12...♗xd4+ wins immediately) 12...♗xd4+ 13.♔g2 ♗e5 14.f4 ♗xb2 15.♗xb2 ♕xb2 16.♘d2 ♕g7 17.♗f3 ♗d7 18.♕e2 0-0-0.

12.c3 e5 13.♘a3 exd4 14.♘c4??

The decisive mistake. Instead 14.♘xd4 ♘e5 15.♕b3 ♕c7 16.♗g5 would allow White to fight his way out, and maybe even to win. But finding the only right path can be very difficult.

14...♕c5 15.b4

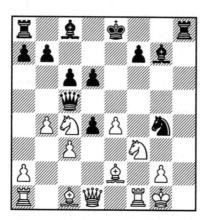

15...♕h5

Whereas Black, aware of the standard queen transfer for an attack on the king, makes use of that idea here. In retrospect, it seems that

White is helping Black to attack the former's king; but in reality, White simply doesn't know about, and doesn't understand, Black's idea.

16.♘h4

16.♘xd6+ ♔f8 and the checks are over, as is the game.

16...♕xh4 17.♗xg4 ♗xg4 18.♕e1 ♕h2+ 19.♔f2 dxc3

19...♖h3! 20.♘xd6+ ♔f8 wins even faster.

20.♗e3 0-0-0 21.♖c1 d5 22.exd5 cxd5 23.♗g5 dxc4 24.♗xd8 ♗d4+ 25.♕e3 ♕f4+ 26.♔e1 ♕xe3#

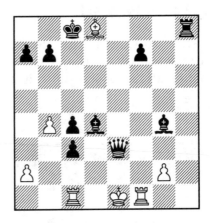

To comment upon White's agony for the last few moves would make no sense.

0-1

20. Carlosthechakal (1983) – NemtsevIgor (2113)

Live Chess on Chess.com 5/9/2015

1.e4 c6 2.d4 d6 3.c4 h6 4.♘c3 g5 5.f4 ♗g7 6.fxg5 ♘d7 7.gxh6 ♘xh6 8.♘f3 ♘f8 9.♗d3

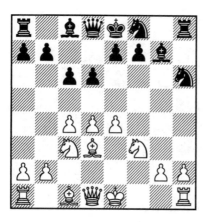

The attentive reader already knows that developing this bishop to d3 isn't good for White, due to the weakness of the d4-pawn.

9...♘e6 10.♗e3

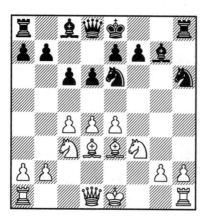

10...♘g4

This is all still "theory" – but known only to you, dear reader! White will keep falling into this trap for a long time to come. I have at least ten similar quick victories. As the saying goes, "the professional approach": we win making practically no original moves!

11.♗g1 ♛b6 12.h3

Well, what can you say – White only *thinks* that he's attacking the g4-knight.

12...♛xb2 13.♖c1 ♛xg2 14.hxg4 ♖xh1 15.♗f1 ♖xg1 16.♘xg1 ♛xg1 17.♘e2 ♛xg4# 0-1

21. Bench – Elshad

Moscow 2012

1.f4 g5

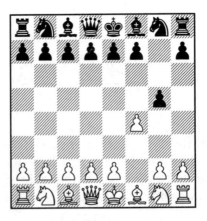

We can go ahead and call this the "Elshad Gambit." This name already occurs in Valerii Chashchikhin's *Manual of Gambit Strategy*

Based on 40 Opening Novelties; I've seen it nowhere else. Its ideas intertwine very strongly with the Elshad System.

2.fxg5 &g7 3.&f3 d6 4.&c3 &d7 5.b3?!

Dubious... I mean, why not try, after all, to occupy the center with pawns, e.g. 5.e4!? h6 6.d4 hxg5 7.&xg5 c6, and the game starts to resemble normal patterns.

5...c6 6.&b2 h6 7.&a4?!

Still another inaccuracy. Of course, White is trading off Black's "dangerous" bishop – but at what cost? How much time has been lost on this operation?!

7...&xb2 8.&xb2 hxg5 9.&xg5

As usually happens in positions where Black's h-pawn is off the board, White can't play 9.h3? because of 9...g4.

9...&e5 10.d4 &g4

10...&a5+!? is decent too: 11.&d2 &xd2+ 12.&xd2 &g4 13.h3 &8f6 14.&g1 &g8! 15.&f3 &e4+ 16.&d3 &ef2+ 17.&d2, and if he so desires, Black may conclude the game by perpetual check.

11.h3 &h5 12.&f3 &8f6 13.&d2

In his zeal to castle queenside, White oversteps the bounds of equality...

13...&e4 14.&f4?

14.&c1 (forced) 14...&a5+ 15.c3 &xc3+ 16.&xc3 &xc3 17.&d1 &xd1 18.&xd1 f5 19.&g1 &e3 20.&d3 &d5 21.g3 a5, with a clear edge for Black.

14...&a5+ 15.&d2 d5 16.0-0-0 &c3 17.a4 &b4 18.&b1?? &a2#:

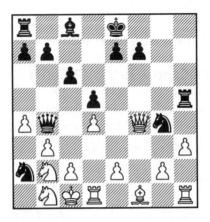

0-1

22. Novichkov – Elshad

7/17/2015

1.e4 c6 2.d4 d6 3.f4 ♘d7 4.♘f3 h6 5.♘c3 g5 6.fxg5 hxg5 7.♗xg5 ♛b6

8.♛c1

When the queen (value = 9 pawns) ends up defending a pawn, it means that, somewhere along the line, White has played something not quite right. The queen is an attacking piece – the strongest one there is. A pawn should be defended by another pawn – or, in the most extreme cases, by a minor piece.

8.b3! ♕a5 9.♕d2 ♘h6 10.♗d3 f6! 11.♗f4 e5 12.♗g3 ♘g4, threatening ...♗h6, which forces White to play 11.♘b1 ♕b6 with a complicated game. It is promising for Black, especially if he is aware of 4-6 different ways of playing these positions. White, on the other hand, knows literally nothing about them.

8...♘h6 9.♗d3 ♘g4 10.♘e2 ♗g7 11.c3 ♘f8 12.♕c2 ♘e6 13.♗d2 c5!

Tearing into the d4-pawn like a wild boar!

14.d5?

Not only a tactical oversight, but also showing an understandable lack of familiarity with the position. Black's reply is plain to see, and also comes up frequently in the Modern Benoni.

14...c4! 15.♗xc4

15.dxe6 ♕f2+ 16.♔d1 ♕xg2 17.exf7+ ♔f8 18.♖g1 ♕xf3 19.♗xc4 ♖h2 leads to much the same thing as in the game.

15...♕f2+ 16.♔d1 ♕xg2 17.♖g1 ♕xf3 18.dxe6 ♗xe6 19.♗xe6 fxe6 20.♕a4+ ♔d8 21.♕a5+ b6 22.♕b5 ♖xh2 0-1

23. V. Bagdasarov – Elshad

7/17/2015

1.e4 d6 2.d4 h6 3.♘c3 ♘d7 4.f4 g5 5.♘f3 ♗g7 6.♗c4 ♘f8 7.fxg5 c6 8.0-0

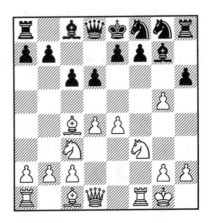

We present three consecutive games starting from this position. Black's stratagem is impressive – luring White into hitting f7!

8...♕b6 9.♗xf7+ ♔xf7 10.♘e5+ ♔e8 11.♕h5+ ♔d8 12.♘f7+ ♔c7 13.♘xh8 ♗xh8

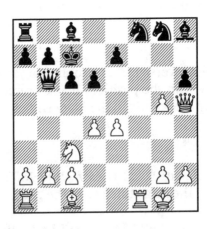

There – all forced, practically! What White failed to consider when launching his "attack" was that the most important spot in the whole position is d4, and that's undefended.

14.♖xf8

Looks like the end. But it is exactly at this point that Black's position springs back up!

14...♗g4! 15.♕f7

On 15.♕xg4? ♗xd4+ 16.♔h1 ♖xf8, all of a sudden it becomes clear that White is the one who is absolutely undeveloped: 17.♗d2 ♕xb2 18.♕d1 ♗xc3 19.♖b1 ♕a3 20.♖b3 ♕a6, and the contest ends in either checkmate or the serious loss of material.

15...♗e6!

As if by magic, it turns out that all of Black's pieces are ideally cooperating with each other, Among other things, the e7-pawn is no longer hanging.

16.♕f1 ♗xd4+ 17.♔h1 ♖xf8 18.♕xf8 hxg5

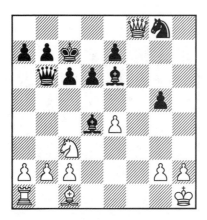

Yes, Black is down the exchange, but White must finish his development somehow.

19.♘e2 ♗f6

Unexpectedly (for White), his queen is now locked out of play.

20.♕e8 ♘h6! 21.♕h5

21.h3 is probably White's last chance here; on the other hand, already some moves back, *Houdini* started showing a serious minus for White. 21...♕f2 22.♕h5 ♗g4! 23.hxg4 ♕xe2 24.♕xh6 ♕e1+ 25.♔h2 ♗e5+ 26.g3 ♗xg3+ 27.♔g2 ♕f2+ 28.♔h1 ♕f1#:

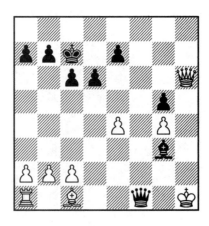

21...♘g4 22.h3 ♘f2+ 23.♔h2 ♗e5+ 24.g3

24...g4

24...♘g4+!! would be the most fitting finish to the attack: 25.hxg4 ♕f2+ 26.♔h1 ♕e1+ 27.♔h2 ♕xe2+ 28.♔h1 ♕xe4+ 29.♔h2 ♗d5 30.♗xg5 ♕g2#:

25.♗f4 ♘xh3 26.♖f1 ♕b5 27.♖e1 ♕c5 28.♖f1 ♕c4 29.♖e1 ♕xe4 30.♕e8 ♗d5 31.♕xe7+ ♔b6 32.♕d8+ ♔a6

0-1

24. Kashlinskaya A. – Elshad

Moscow (rapid), n.d.

1.e4 d6 2.d4 h6 3.♘c3 ♘d7 4.f4 g5 5.♘f3 ♗g7 6.♗c4 ♘f8 7.fxg5 c6 8.0-0 ♛b6 9.♗xf7+ ♚xf7 10.♘e5+ ♚e8 11.♛h5+ ♚d8 12.♘f7+ ♚c7 13.♘xh8 ♗xh8 14.♖xf8 ♗g4 15.♛f7 ♗e6 16.♛f1 ♗xd4+ 17.♚h1 ♖xf8 18.♛xf8 hxg5

Only here does White spring her improvement.

19.a4!? &f6 20.a5?

She had to find 20.e5!! &xe5 21.a5 ♛b4 (unfortunately, Black's queen can't go to f2 because of &xg5) 22.&e3 ♛h4 (22...♛xb2?? 23.♖b1 ♛xc3 24.&xa7 &c8 25.&b6+ ♚d7 26.♛d8+ ♚e6 27.♛xg8+, and White wins) 23.&g1 &c4 24.h3 &xc3 25.bxc3 &d5 26.♚h2 ♛e4 27.♛f3 ♛xc2, and the whole struggle still lies ahead.

20...♛f2

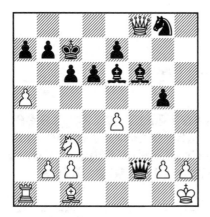

It's very easy to lose one's way here. Mate is threatened on the first rank.

21.&xg5 &h3 22.gxh3??

22.♖g1 (forced) 22...&xg2+ 23.♖xg2 ♛f1+ 24.♖g1 ♛f3+ would probably lead to a draw.

22...♛f3+ 23.♚g1 &d4+ 24.&e3 &xe3#

(see diagram next page)

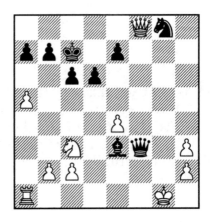

0-1

25. Sh. Mkoyan – Elshad

7/17/2015

1.e4 d6 2.d4 h6 3.♘c3 ♘d7 4.f4 g5 5.♘f3 ♗g7 6.♗c4 ♘f8
7.fxg5 c6 8.0-0 ♕b6 9.♗xf7+ ♔xf7 10.♘e5+ ♔e8 11.♕h5+
♔d8 12.♘f7+ ♔c7 13.♘xh8 ♗xh8 14.♖xf8 ♗g4 15.♕f7 ♗e6
16.♕f1 ♗xd4+ 17.♔h1 ♖xf8 18.♕xf8 hxg5

Shagen is a friend of Elshad's and mine, with a Ph.D. in Chemistry. Some years ago he showed up in Sokolniki Park as a middling 2000-level player. But now he has matured into a solid master. And up to this day, he had been the "refuter" of the Elshad System. Let's thank him for his efforts – that's how theory moves ahead!

19.♘e2!?

And here's his novelty!

19...♗f6 20.c3?!

Once again, he has to play 20.e5!!, with equal chances in the coming struggle: 20...♗xe5 21.♗xg5 ♕xb2 22.♖e1 ♕xa2 23.♗xe7 ♘xe7 24.♕xe7+ ♗d7.

20...♕f2 21.♘g1 ♕e1

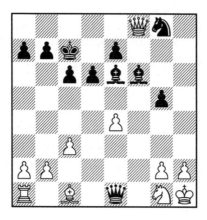

I don't see how White could untangle himself on his first rank.

22.b3 ♕xc3 23.♖b1 ♕c2 0-1

26. N. Zhadanov – Elshad

1.e4 c6 2.d4 d6 3.c4 ♘d7 4.♘c3 h6 5.♗e3

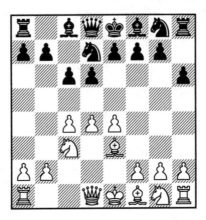

In my comments to the previous games, I noted more than once that this bishop development tends to be premature. This becomes especially clear when White has to take on g5 with the bishop, losing a tempo. Also, this bishop regularly comes under fire from the knight when the latter reaches g4.

5...g5 6.♗d3 ♕a5 7.♘ge2

Now, here's progress – at least, from White's point of view. Nikolai Zhadanov is a good positional player and a FIDE Master. He can see that, were his knight to come out to f3, it would be harassed by the g-pawn.

7...a6 8.0-0 b5!?

A complete change of scenery. This is one way that the originator differs from those of us who merely employ his system.

9.f4 b4 10.♘b1 ♗g7 11.fxg5 hxg5 12.♖f5

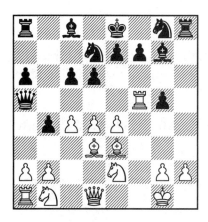

The critical point in the game. The position is original – even for this most esoteric of openings. If the black queen retreats now, his whole conception collapses.

12...♘e5!?

12...c5!? looks like a most convincing alternative: 13.♖xg5 ♗f6 14.♖f5 ♘h6 15.♗xh6 (15.♖f4?! cxd4 16.♘xd4 ♗g5 17.♖f3 ♘g4 18.♗xg5 ♛e5!!:

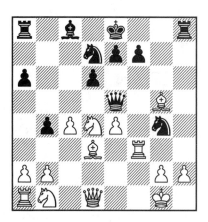

19.♗f4 ♛xd4+ 20.♔h1 ♘de5 21.♗xe5 ♛xe5 22.♛g1 ♖xh2+ 23.♛xh2 ♛xh2#) 15...♖xh6 16.♘d2 ♛c7 17.♘f3 cxd4 18.♛d2 ♖h8 19.♖f1 ♘e5 20.♘xe5 ♗xe5 21.g3 ♗xf5 22.exf5 b3 23.a3 d5 24.cxd5 ♛c5.

13.♖xg5 ♗h6 14.♖xg8+?

14.dxe5!? ♗xg5 15.♗xg5 ♕c5+ 16.♔h1 ♕xe5 17.♗f4 ♕xb2 18.♘d2 ♗g4, with a complex game not susceptible to exact analysis. I, of course, would choose Black.

14...♖xg8 15.♗xh6 ♘f3+ 16.♔f2 ♘xh2 17.♗f4 ♘g4+ 18.♔e1

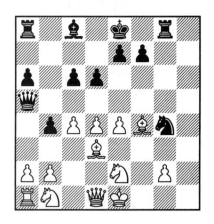

18...e5!

Simple and strong!

19.dxe5 dxe5 20.♗g3 ♗e6

20...♘e3! 21.♕b3 ♘xg2+ 22.♔d1 ♕c5 23.♘d2 ♖xg3 24.♘xg3 ♗g4+ 25.♔c1 ♕f2 26.♕xb4 ♕xg3 27.♕b7 ♖d8 28.♕xc6+ ♗d7 29.♕h6 ♕e1+ 30.♔c2 ♘e3+ 31.♔c3 ♕xa1−+.

21.♔d2??

This loses. 21.♘d2 is obligatory: 21...0-0-0 22.♘b3 ♕c7, with an ongoing attack.

21...♖d8 22.♔c2 ♘e3+

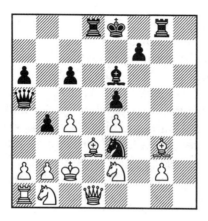

0-1

27. Panteleyev – Elshad

Moscow 2001

1.e4 d6 2.d4 ♘d7 3.♘c3 c6 4.f4 g5

Turns out that you can play it this way, too. And why not? The ideas in Elshad's System intertwine; meanwhile, your opponents have practically no chance of preparing for this sort of game.

5.fxg5 ♗g7 6.♘f3 ♘f8

Panteleyev is a very strong Moscow candidate master. Neverthe-less, after coming up against a surprise like this, he plays several moves that he would not have made had he reached this position a second or a third time. Why does this happen? Several explana-tions are possible. First of all, such play from Black almost begs for a refutation, so it's a question of psychology. Secondly, there is an un-willingness to believe that something like this is even possible, which gives rise to an underestimation of Black's possibilities. Thirdly, the positions that arise are so complex and unusual that it is, in principle, very difficult to grasp what's going on while the clock is ticking. And this means that, fourthly, Elshad's System is especially effective when playing either rapid or blitz chess. There, your opponent has almost no time to figure out your intentions; he'll be making superficial moves based on general considerations. It is here that surprises await him.

7.a4 a5 8.♗c4 h6

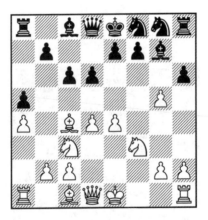

Still, I have to warn those players who start playing this open-ing for Black, that until White castles, he has the rather unpleasant reply 9.♖f1.

9.gxh6

Let's see: 9.♖f1! ♕b6 10.♗xf7+ ♔xf7 11.♘e5+ ♔e8 12.♕h5+ ♔d8 13.♘f7+ ♔c7 14.♘xh8 ♗xh8 15.♕e8! ♕xd4 16.♕xf8. The difference between this game and the one with Kashlinskaya is that now the white king feels safer in the center. Compare for yourself.

9....♘xh6 10.♘g5?!

Pretty superficial, since the f7-pawn is defended securely by the h6-knight.

10...♕b6!

Falling upon White's Achilles' heel – the d4-pawn!

11.d5?

But this is just wrong. Is it because everyone, from beginner to grandmaster, plays into it (see Game 65, Naumkin–Nemtsev)? This pawn "break" creates not a single threat for White, but all sorts of dark-square weaknesses in his camp.

11...♘g6 12.dxc6 bxc6 13.♕d3?! ♘e5 14.♕e2 ♘hg4

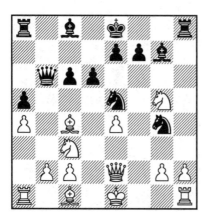

Black's offensive array is one that we see quite often. We already know that, in such positions, White doesn't have the move h2-h3, as the h-pawn is pinned to the h1-rook. Now Black threatens a capture on c4 followed by check with the queen on f2.

15.♗b3 ♗a6 16.♗xf7+ ♔d8

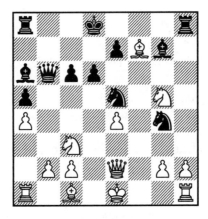

This king sidestep shatters White's illusions of counterplay.

Black might also just snip off the bishop: 16...♘xf7 17.♕xg4 ♘xg5 18.♕xg5 (18.♗xg5? ♕xb2−+) 18...♖xh2!! 19.♖xh2 ♗xc3+ 20.bxc3 ♕g1+ 21.♔d2 ♕f2+ 22.♔d1 ♕e2#:

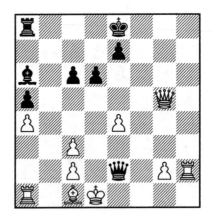

17.♕d2 ♖f8

17...♖xh2−+ (18.♖xh2 ♕g1#) is what Elshad played in other games when he reached this position, but in this game he plays it differently.

18.♘e6+ ♔d7 19.♘xf8+ ♖xf8 20.h3 ♗h6

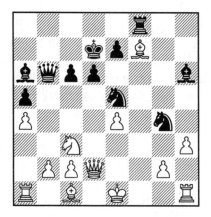

Nowhere to run to, nowhere to go – White resigned.

0-1

28. Stepurko – Elshad

Moscow 2004

1.f4 h6 2.d4 d6 3.e4 g5 4.fxg5 hxg5 5.♗xg5 c6 6.♘f3 ♕b6 7.♘c3 ♖h5

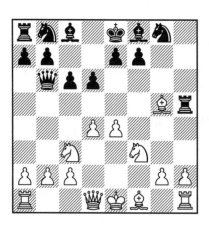

Chapter 1

Elshad's opponent in this game is very well known as a blitz player in Moscow chess circles. I have my own history with Stepurko. Some ten years ago, I dropped in at Sokolniki Park to play a little chess. I was wearing expensive clothes; so he figured his "client" had arrived, and decided to make some money off me. Since we didn't know each other, he thought that I wouldn't give him any trouble; and in this sweet little voice, he grabbed me by the elbow, and started to talk me into playing "the most intellectual game." He said that he would show me wondrous things over the board, and even offered me odds: I would have 5 minutes for the game, and he would get 3. I decided to teach him a lesson: after all, I did know a little about him, as I'd been watching his games. We sat down to play, and right away I started crushing him. He could win only a couple of games the whole evening. The final score was plus-18 in my favor. And when it started getting really dark, so that you couldn't make out the squares on the board (we were playing in summertime, in the open air) – well, now he understood that he had become a "client" himself; so he started to swear a blue streak at me.

And that's how a fellow can go quickly from "wondrous" to "garbage." As for Stepurko, he always plays it out to the end – I'll give him that. In later years, more than once I offered him a chance to take his revenge, but he never played me again. In the following game, he never manages to shake the foundations of strategy of the Elshad System. More than that, he made all of White's typical mistakes.

8.b3 &g7

8...&g4!? also deserves attention. I suggest that you study that move on your own.

9.&e3 &f6 10.h3 &g4

This is seen in every other game played with the Elshad, so there's no point in discussing it yet again.

11.♗g1 ♘d7

11...♕a5!? 12.♕d3 ♘a6 13.a3 ♘c5! (how many different kinds of tactics we find in this position!) 14.♕c4 ♘xe4 15.b4 ♕c7 16.♘xe4 d5 17.♕e2 dxe4 18.♕xe4 a5!.

12.♘a4 ♕c7 13.♘h2

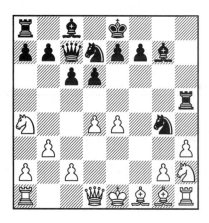

Trying to untangle his pile of pieces on the kingside.

13...♘gf6 14.♘g4 ♕a5+ 15.♔f2?

15.c3 b5 16.♘xf6+ ♘xf6 17.♘b2 ♕xc3+ 18.♕d2 ♕xd2+ 19.♔xd2 ♘xe4+ 20.♔c2 ♘g3 21.♖h2, and White's position lies in ruins.

15...♘xg4+ 16.♕xg4 ♗xd4+ 17.♔e2 ♘f6

(see diagram next page)

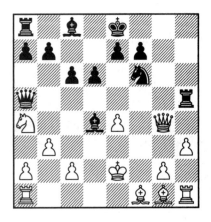

0-1

29. GM Rinat Jumabayev – Elshad

Moscow 2012

1.e4 d6 2.d4 h6 3.♘c3 c6 4.♗e3

This move is premature if White doesn't plan on castling queen-side.

4...♘d7 5.f4 g5

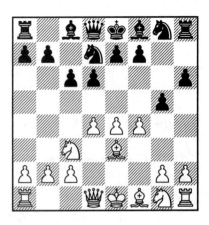

This is what happens after the inexact ♗c1-e3. If White now takes twice on g5, he clearly loses a tempo, since instead of the bishop move he could have made some other developing move.

6.fxg5 hxg5!

Strongest. Not only does Black win that extra tempo, but he doesn't give White the opportunity (say, after ...♗f8-g7) to change the course of the struggle with g5-g6, for example 6...♗g7 7.g6:

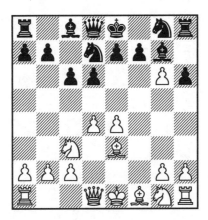

7...fxg6 8.♕d3 ♘f8 9.♘f3 ♘f6 10.h3 g5 11.0-0-0, and although Black does have a decent game, the light squares around his king remain weak.

7.♗xg5 ♕b6 8.♖b1

When I'm teaching my young students, I explain a move like this as follows: if the rook (worth 5 points) has to protect a pawn (worth 1), that means that, somewhere, White has made a mistake: A strong piece should not be tied down to holding a pawn. Additionally, this rook is now immobile, since if it moves away Black will capture on b2. A pawn should be protected by a pawn.

8...♗g7 9.♘f3 ♘f8 10.♗e2 ♘h6!

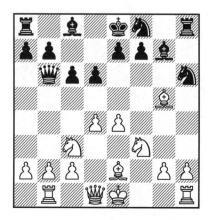

Just so! Black could just as well get to g4 via f6, but, all else being equal, the g7-bishop stays active on the long diagonal.

11.0-0

11.h3 ♘e6 12.♗e3 ♘g4!. A well-known trick in Elshad's System: the rook pawn is pinned, so White doesn't have hxg4.

11...♗g4

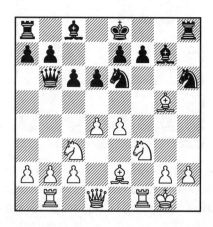

11...♘e6!? is stronger, the point being that this move would create a direct threat to take the bishop and then the d4-pawn. If 12.♗e3, then 12...♘g4! 13.♗f2 ♘xf2 14.♖xf2 ♘xd4.

12.♗e3 ♘e6 13.♘a4 ♛a5 14.c4 ♛h5

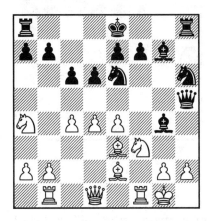

15.h3?

A mistake, allowing Black to launch a crushing attack. How exactly should White play? With 15.♛b3!, hitting the b7-pawn. This would have highlighted the bishop's absence from c8. Then 15...b6 16.♘c3 ♗xf3 17.♗xf3 ♛h4 18.♖bd1 ♘g5 19.♗xg5 ♛xg5 20.e5 dxe5 21.♗xc6+ ♚f8 22.♘e4 ♛g6 23.♗xa8 would be quite bad for Black.

15...♗xh3!

Now Black has a clear advantage.

16.♘h2

If White snaps off the bishop, he suffers a quick defeat: 16.gxh3? ♛xh3 17.♚f2 ♘g4+ 18.♚e1 ♘xe3 19.♛d3 ♘f4 20.♛xe3 ♘g2+ 21.♚d2 ♘xe3 22.♚xe3 c5−+.

16...♛g6

Threatening mate on g2.

17.♗f3

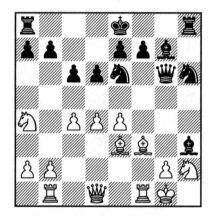

17...♖g8

Simple and strong. There is another possibility, too, which the computer says is even stronger: 17...c5! 18.d5 (18.dxc5 ♗e5 19.♕d2 ♕g3 20.cxd6 ♕xh2+ 21.♔f2 ♘g4+ 22.♗xg4 ♕xg2+ 23.♔e1 ♕xf1#; 18.♖f2 cxd4 19.♗c1 ♗e5 20.♘f1 ♖g8 21.c5 dxc5 22.b4 c4 23.♘c5 ♘xc5 24.bxc5 ♘g4 – all of White's attempts to distract Black from the attack on his king come to naught) 18...♘d4 19.♖f2 ♗e5 20.♘f1 ♘xf3+ 21.♕xf3 (21.♖xf3 ♕xg2#) 21...♗g4, and the queen is lost.

18.♖f2 ♗h8 19.d5 ♘g5 20.♘c3 ♗d7!?

Notice how the bishop shuttles back and forth. Now Black threatens ...♘h3.

21.♔f1 ♘xf3 22.♕xf3

As pointed out by IMs Pavel Dvalishvili and Evgeny Dragomaretsky, who were kibitzing the game, 22.gxf3 is the only move to prolong resistance. But then 22...♗e5 23.♘e2 f5 is still bad for White.

22...♘g4 23.♘xg4 ♗xg4 24.♕f4 ♗e5 25.♕h6 ♕xh6

25...♖h8!:

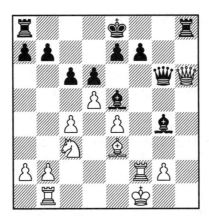

That would have been a fitting conclusion to this game!

26.♗xh6 ♖h8,

And the grandmaster resigned. **0-1**

30. Khorsun – M. Amannazarov

1.e4 c6 2.d4 d6 3.♘c3 ♘d7 4.♗e3 ♕a5 5.♕d2 h6 6.f4 g5 7.♘f3

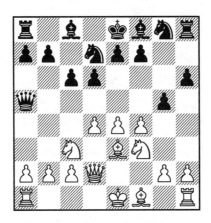

7...gxf4

This is good, but it's not the only possibility in the diagram position:

7...♗g7 is in the spirit of this system. Black need not fear the loss of his g5-pawn, since taking it would free Black's hands to fight for the dark squares.

7...♘gf6 is the strongest. The general "rule" in Elshad's System when White's dark-squared bishop comes out to e3, is: bring your own knight out to f6 at once! The idea is to immediately create the positional threat of ...♘f6-g4xe3, trading off one of the defenders of White's central dark squares. After 7...♘gf6, White has three choices:

1) 8.e5 is a timely and most unpleasant possibility for Black. Nevertheless, it all eventually works out for the second player: 8... gxf4 (8...dxe5 9.fxe5 ♘g4 10.e6 fxe6 11.♗d3 ♘df6 clearly favors White; 8...♘g4 9.exd6 exd6 10.0-0-0 ♗g7 leads to a hard fight with equal chances) 9.♗xf4 dxe5 10.♘xe5 ♘xe5 11.♗xe5 ♗e6 12.♗xf6 exf6:

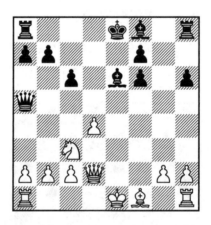

In this position, the advantage most likely now belongs to Black – although it is also possible that White has not played the strongest moves available.

2) 8.h3 g4. A standard blow in this opening. What is White to do? If 9.hxg4, then 9...♘xg4 and once again Black threatens to eliminate White's valuable bishop.

3) 8.fxg5 is the most principled try: 8...♘g4 9.♗f4 hxg5 10.♘xg5 ♗g7 11.h3 ♘f8 12.♗c4 ♗e6 13.♘xe6 ♘xe6 14.♗xe6 fxe6 15.0-0-0 e5 16.dxe5 ♘xe5:

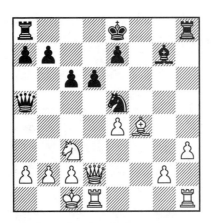

From my viewpoint, Black has full compensation for the pawn. The e5 point is very important!

7...g4 is also quite possible: 8.♘h4 ♗g7 9.e5 dxe5 (once a white pawn appears at either e5 or c5, it must be eliminated at once; otherwise White will take on d6 himself, and we don't want that) 10.dxe5 ♘c5 with dynamic equality. Black's pieces pass through the e6 square on their way to their fighting posts, and if White ever plays f4-f5, then the e5-pawn is weakened.

8.♗xf4 ♗g7 9.♗e2 ♘f8

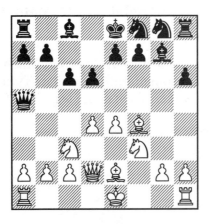

Chapter 1

The standard knight transfer to better squares – either to e6, to put pressure on the d4-pawn, or to g6, for a direct attack on the white king.

9...♛b6. Just a note: from b6, the queen pressures b2 and looks obliquely at the g1 square, where the white king may sit.

10.0-0 ♞g6

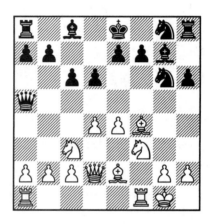

10...♞e6. This, too, gives Black an outstanding game: 11.♗e3 ♞f6 12.h3 ♜g8 and Black's attack shouldn't be underestimated. Or 12... ♗d7 13.b4 ♛c7 14.b5 ♜g8 15.bxc6 bxc6, and here White's queenside "play" is over before it begins, while Black is just getting started with his g-file attack.

11.♗g3 ♞f6 12.♜ad1 ♞h5 13.♗f2 ♞hf4 14.♗e3 ♞xe2+ 15.♛xe2 ♗e6 16.a3

The black pawn on h6 prevents the white knight from getting to g5! White has to play something – but what? Trying to play on the queenside doesn't bother Black in the least (16.d5? ♗d7).

16...♛h5 17.♛f2 ♗c4 18.♜fe1 0-0

A minor inaccuracy. Murad (who played Black) and I analyzed this game afterward; I was sitting in the legendary chair where Viktor Korchnoi once sat. I remember that, at that moment, our opinions diverged. How do you attack along the g-file, asked Murad; while I tried to figure out the exact attack after ...♖g8. And I did find it:

18...♖g8! 19.♘e2 (19.b3 ♗a6 20.♘e2 ♗xe2 21.♖xe2 0-0-0 22.c4 ♔b8 23.b4 f5 24.exf5 ♕xf5 25.b5 cxb5 26.cxb5 ♕xb5 27.♖b2 ♕a6 28.♖db1 b6) 19...♗xe2 20.♕xe2 ♕g4 21.♕d3 (21.c4 ♕xe4):

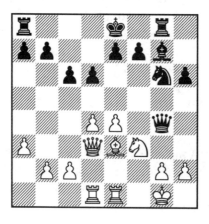

A critical moment for the whole offensive. Black has too many pieces arrayed on the g-file – so he needs to clear out the file! Finding the next move is difficult – but *Houdini* finds it in one second: 21...♗xd4!! – the bishop is attacked three times! Now:

1) 22.♘xd4 ♘f4 (attacking the queen and threatening mate on g2) 23.♕f1 ♘xg2 24.♔h1 ♘xe1 25.♖xe1 ♕xe4+ 26.♕f3 ♕xf3+ 27.♘xf3 h5∓:

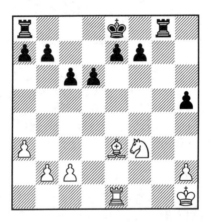

The evaluation of this ending is very simple: Black is much better, with a material plus (rook and three pawns for bishop and knight), plus a positional advantage consisting of the fact that Black can carry out his plan – advancing the pawns to their queening squares – while White can't undertake any sort of action to make use of his "advantage" in the number of pieces. I would like to quote what should be a general principle of theory: the fewer pieces remain on the board, the stronger the rook and pawns become against the two minor pieces.

2) 22.g3 ♗xb2. A purely computer move; however, at this point, it's very easy to find the idea to explain it: first of all, he takes yet another pawn; and second, he grabs the e5 square! 23.♖f1 ♘e5 24.♘xe5 ♗xe5 25.♗d4 ♗xd4+ 26.♕xd4 h5∓:

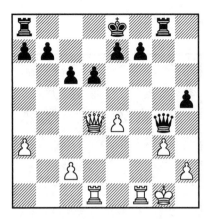

Black has a clear advantage, thanks not just to his two extra pawns, but also to his continuing attack against the white king. The ...h5-h4 push is coming.

3) 22.♖d2 e5 23.♘xe5 ♗xe5 24.♖f2 0-0-0∓.

4) 22.♗xd4 ♘e5 23.♕f1 ♘xf3+ 24.♔h1 (24.♕xf3 ♕xf3 – simple: take the queens off) 24...♘xe1 25.♖xe1 f6−+:

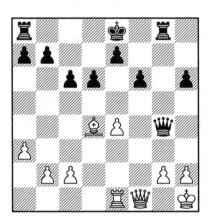

White is down the exchange and a pawn; on the "other" hand, his position is worse!

19.♘e2 ♗xe2 20.♖xe2

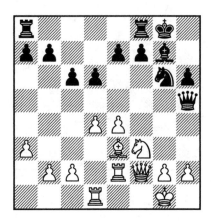

20...b6

Now that Black has castled, there's another opportunity for him: 20...f5!? 21.exf5 ♖xf5 22.♖ee1 ♖af8.

21.b4 a5 22.c3 axb4 23.axb4 ♖a3

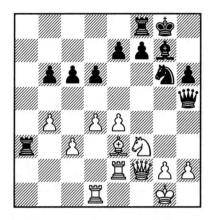

This is the last important moment in this game. White had to defend his d4- and c3-pawns to the end. Now Black will break into White's rear area; and even though the first player could have defended better at some point, in general this kind of pressure cannot be borne successfully, even by very strong players.

24.c4 ♖fa8 25.c5 bxc5 26.dxc5 dxc5 27.♗xc5 ♘e5 28.♖e3 ♖a1 29.♖ee1 ♖8a2 30.♕g3 ♖xd1 31.♖xd1 ♘xf3+ 32.gxf3 ♔h7 33.h3 e6 34.♔f1 ♕e5 35.♕xe5 ♗xe5 36.♖d7 ♔g6 37.♗f2 ♖b2 38.♖b7 ♗c3 39.♖b6??

An awful blunder, of course. But I can just imagine how profusely White must have been sweating in this game. In such games, mistakes are the consequence of great pressure in an unfamiliar situation.

39...♖xf2+ 40.♔xf2 ♗d4+ 41.♔e2 ♗xb6 0-1

Chapter 2

White Builds a Fortress With g2-g3 and ♗g2

31. MastaK (2856) – MASTER-GURU (2851)

05/26/2014

1.c4 d6 2.♘c3 c6 3.♘f3 ♘d7 4.g3

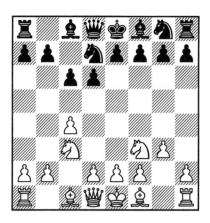

A popular system in which White constructs a very "safe" little home for his king. But it is in just this construction that White encounters big problems. Often, he ends up castling queenside.

4...h6 5.♗g2 g5

It's not too late to play h2-h4. On the other hand, even after that move Black has prospects for a powerful attack.

6.d4 ♗g7 7.e4 ♞f8 8.♗e3

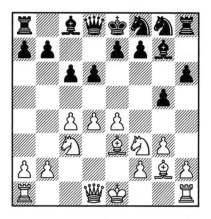

8...♞e6

8...♞f6! is stronger, as it creates the threat of this knight's jumping to g4, followed by exchanging it for the e3-bishop. Since this whole opening is built around a dark-square strategy, the dark-squared bishops have great significance in the ensuing play. White would have to play h2-h3 in order to deter our knight from going there, but that gives Black a further "nail" on which to hang his kingside attack later on.

9.♕d2

9.d5 ♞f8 10.c5±. This leads to an advantage for White, but Black's resources are not yet exhausted. Elshad himself, the author of this system, put forward a good analogy: "If you build a house and you're laying the roof tiles, they all have to line up. If you lay down a different-sized tile, then your roof will leak. In this opening, Black must constantly be laying down 'his' tiles, while White will struggle the whole game to demonstrate his idea."

9...♞f6

And now, where to castle? That is one of White's universal questions in this opening. On the kingside?! Even a cursory glance makes it evident how dangerous that is.

10.0-0-0 ♘g4

Simple and strong.

11.d5 ♘xe3 12.fxe3

12.♛xe3:

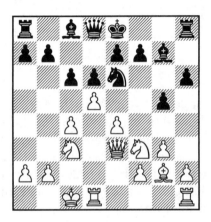

12...♘c5!. A very important point. As a rule, in this opening it's not good for Black to take the d5-pawn with his c-pawn. His formula for success is as follows: the c6-pawn should always be kept in place, so as not to allow White's pieces into either b5 or d5. Or the pawn may go to c5 to fix the pawn structure – especially the dark-square diagonal a1-h8.

12...♘c5 13.♘d4 ♗g4 14.♗f3

This was a mistake, but not everyone is up to making an exchange sacrifice. White should play 14.dxc6, with some survival chances.

14...♗xf3 15.♘xf3

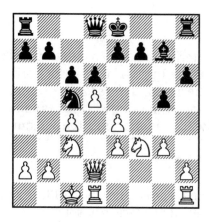

Even the emotionless computer rates this position clearly in White's favor. In human terms, though, Black's advantage consists of several factors:

1) His powerful dark-squared bishop – the same sort he enjoys in the Sicilian Dragon.

2) The possibility of attacking the white king on the queenside with ...♕a5 or ...♕b6.

3) White has doubled pawns; in case of a transition into an ending, they will prove to be a serious deficiency in White's position.

4) And last but not least, Black has a clear plan – to attack. Meanwhile, White has no play at all. It is a typical mirage for White in this opening: all of his pieces aim at the center and space has been seized – and yet, it's practically *Zugzwang*.

15...♕b6

15...b5!?. One should also keep this possibility in mind. It's very strong, although not quite in the spirit of this opening. Nevertheless, we insist that, if you must choose between playing a strong move or playing in the spirit of this system, then play the strong move: 16.dxc6 (16.cxb5 cxb5 17.♔b1 b4 18.♘e2 ♘xe4 19.♕c2 ♘f2) 16...bxc4 17.♔b1 ♖b8.

16.♘d4 a5

This is just a battering ram, which is quite usual in positions with opposite-side castling. In general, the chief principle for playing such positions is the motto, *"Who's faster?"* In such situations, you have to assault the opposing king with pieces and pawns. And, inasmuch as here only Black is attacking, the outcome is foreordained.

17.♘f5 ♗e5 18.h4 g4

Simple and strong. The engine advises Black to play ...g4xh3 *e.p.* with ...♕b4 to follow, but there is absolutely no reason to open a second front. In our case, the game is a one-way street.

19.h5 a4 20.♖hf1

This move cannot be called a mistake, because there's really nothing else to suggest.

20...a3 21.b3 ♘xb3+ 22.axb3 ♕xb3 23.♘d4 ♗xd4 24.exd4 a2

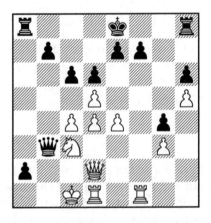

0-1

32. GM M. Brodsky – I. Nemtsev

Chess Planet 2014

This game was played over the Internet. Many players will recognize themselves in this book. And so: a game against a grandmaster.

1.d4 d6 2.♘f3 c6 3.g3

Developing the bishop to g2 now is even worse than taking control of the center. The point is that in Elshad's System, Black goes for an attack on the kingside castled position. The g3-pawn and f3-knight thus become targets for the pawn storm. True, it does seem to White that his king is very securely covered.

3...♘d7 4.♗g2 h6 5.0-0 g5 6.c4 ♗g7 7.♘c3 ♘f8

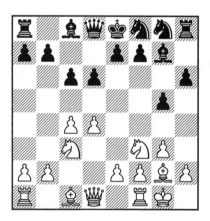

The knight follows the standard path to e6, in order to induce White into advancing with d4-d5.

8.e4

8.d5 c5 9.e4 ♘g6 10.a3 g4 11.♘d2 h5 12.b4 ♗xc3; 8.e3 ♘g6 9.b3 g4 10.♘h4 (10.♘d2 h5 11.♗b2 h4 12.♖c1 ♕a5 13.a3 ♕h5 14.b4 hxg3 15.hxg3 ♕h2#):

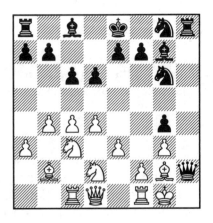

10...♘xh4 11.gxh4 ♛a5! with the idea of ...♛h5, with an attack.

8...♘e6 9.d5

White has to think about the threat of ...g5-g4!, e.g. 9.♖e1 g4 10.♘h4 ♘xd4; or 9.♗e3 ♘f6 10.h3 g4 11.hxg4 ♘xg4.

9...♘f8 10.♛c2 c5

10...♘g6 11.c5.

11.♖e1 ♘g6 12.b3

12.e5 ♘xe5 13.♘xe5 ♗xe5 14.f4 gxf4 15.gxf4 ♗d4+ 16.♔h1 ♘f6.

12...g4!

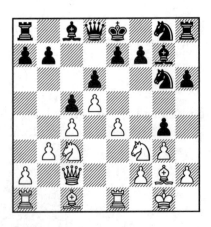

If 12...♗g4, then 13.♗b2 ♗xf3 14.♗xf3 ♘e5 15.♗g2 g4.

13.♘d2 h5

At this point, the fellow with the white pieces started to understand that Black's assault along the h-file was very dangerous. Theory recommends that an attack on the wing should be countered by a break in the center. But how? The e5 square is firmly under Black's control.

14.♗b2

14.f4 gxf3 15.♘xf3 h4.

14...h4 15.♘d1 ♔f8

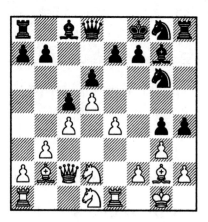

Elshad's favorite move. I could have played 15...♗e5, of course, irretrievably taking over the e5 square.

16.♗xg7+ ♔xg7 17.♕c3+ ♘f6 18.♘e3 ♖h5

Here was White's last chance to alter the course of events, by playing 19.f4.

19.a3

19.f4 gxf3 20.♗xf3 ♖g5 21.♘f5+ ♗xf5 22.exf5 ♘e5 23.g4 ♘xf3+ (23...♘exg4?? 24.♘e4) 24.♕xf3 ♖xg4+ 25.♔h1 ♕h8 26.♖g1 ♔f8

27.☖xg4 ♘xg4 28.☖g1 ♘e5 29.♕g2 a5 30.a4 ♔e8 31.♘e4 h3. But here too, Black has the better of it: 32.♕g3 ♔d7.

19...♕h8 20.b4 ♘e5

20...b6!:

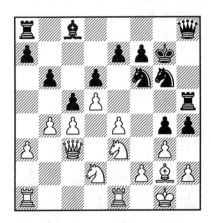

Squashing any hope of counterplay for White – and after this, of course, a mating attack by Black (21.bxc5 bxc5, etc.).

21.♘f5+?

21.bxc5!? hxg3 22.hxg3 ♗d7 23.cxd6 exd6 24.☖ab1 b6.

21...♗xf5 22.exf5 hxg3 23.hxg3

23.♕xg3 ☖xf5 24.bxc5 ♘h5 25.♕c3 (25.♕h4 ♘f4 26.♕xh8+ ☖xh8 27.cxd6 exd6 28.♘f1 *[28.☖e3]* 28...♘h3+ 29.♗xh3 ♘f3+ 30.♔h1 ♘xe1 31.♗xg4 ♘c2 32.♗xf5 ♘xa1) 25...♘f4.

23...☖h2

Tripling major pieces on the h-file is even stronger: 23...♕h7! 24.☖xe5 ☖h8 25.♔f1 dxe5 26.♕xe5 ♕xf5 27.♕xf5 ☖xf5 28.bxc5 ♘d7 29.♘b3 ♘e5.

24.bxc5 ☖xg2+ 25.♔xg2 ♕h3+ 26.♔g1 ☖h8

White Builds a Fortress with g2-g3 and ♗g2

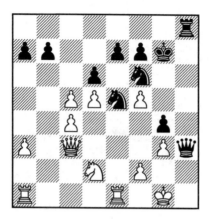

A standard mate, which made White's hair stand on end.

0-1

33. So* (2637) – Nemtsev_Igor (2718)

3/27/2015

1.♘f3 c6 2.d4 d6 3.c4 ♘d7 4.g3 h6 5.♗g2 g5 6.0-0 ♗g7 7.♘c3 ♘f8 8.e4 ♘e6

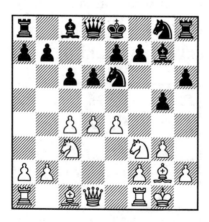

You might call this the "theoretical position"!

---

* Almost certainly not GM Wesley So – Ed.

9.d5 ♘f8 10.♘d4

An attempt to exploit c6.

10...c5

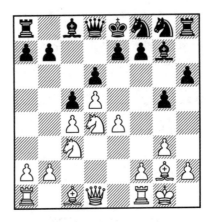

In this situation, this is right – Black has to close up the position and play for the e5 square!

11.♘f5 ♗xf5

11...♗xc3!. A totally new idea in this opening, as yet not tested in practice. I recommend it (12.bxc3 ♘g6).

12.exf5 ♘d7 13.♖e1 ♗e5 14.♔h1 ♘gf6 15.♕d3 g4!

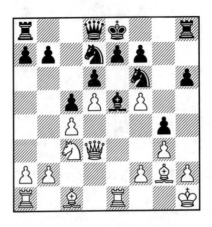

It's important to understand why this move was made. Here we see an example of the qualitative superiority of the g4-pawn over the pawns covering White's castled king, a typical aggressive theme in our opening. In some cases, it's followed by the forward drive of the h-pawn.

16.b3 h5 17.♗b2 h4

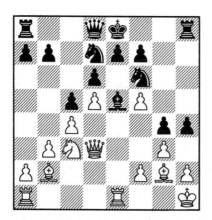

This is a lot like my Brodsky game, no?

18.♘a4 hxg3 19.♗xe5?

Alternatives don't save White, either: 19.fxg3 ♖h5 20.♔g1 ♕c7 21.♖e2 0-0-0 22.a3 ♖dh8 23.♗h1 ♗xb2 24.♘xb2 ♘e5–+:

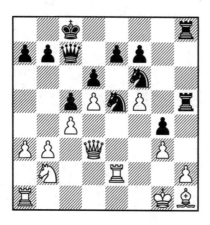

Compare the light-squared white bishop with Black's knight on e5! Or the two kings!!

19...♖xh2+ 20.♔g1 ♞xe5

20...gxf2+!! 21.♔xh2 (21.♔xf2 ♞xe5 22.♖xe5 dxe5–+) 21...fxe1♕ 22.♖xe1 ♞xe5–+.

21.♖xe5 dxe5 22.fxg3 ♖h5

The rest is simple.

23.♖e1 ♕d6 24.♕e3 ♖c8 25.♕xe5 ♔f8 26.♞c3 ♕xe5 27.♖xe5 ♞e8 28.♖e4 ♞f6 29.♖f4 ♔g7 30.♞e4 ♞xe4 31.♖xg4+ ♞g5 0-1

34. Yaroslav_2003 (2362) – Nemtsev_Igor (2788)

3/28/2015

1.d4 c6 2.c4 d6 3.♞c3 ♞d7 4.g3 h6 5.♗g2 g5 6.h4

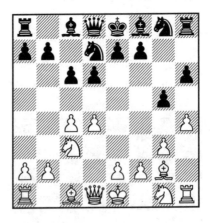

6...g4!

Black's position is so filled with possibilities that here 6...gxh4 and even 6...♕b6 are totally possible. I recommend that you immerse yourself in these complexities on your own.

6...♛b6 7.hxg5 ♗g7!? 8.gxh6 ♗xd4 9.e3 ♗xc3+ 10.bxc3 ♖xh6 11.♖xh6 ♘xh6 12.♛h5 ♘g8 13.♛h8 ♘df6:

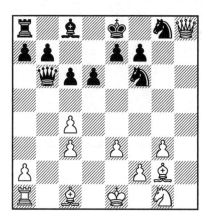

White's position amounts to nothing more than an assortment of weak pawns.

7.e4 h5

7...♗g7!?:

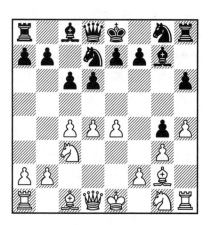

8.♛xg4 ♗xd4 9.♛e2 ♘e5 10.♘f3 ♗g4.

8.♘ge2 ♗g7 9.0-0 ♘f8 10.d5?!

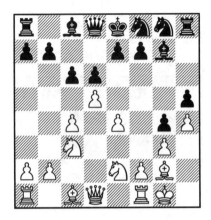

In the style of GM Naumkin. White thinks that he is attacking in the center, but in reality he's merely surrendering the dark squares all over the board!

10...c5

10...♞g6 11.♗e3 c5 12.♞f4 ♞e5

11.f4?

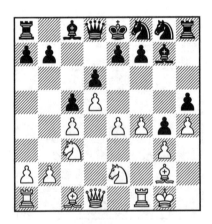

Pressing on with his doomed strategy. I'm sure that White thought he was "attacking" my king.

11...gxf3! 12.♗xf3 ♘g6 13.♗g2 ♗e5 14.♔h2

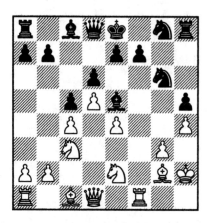

Although this is a blunder, White would still be in obvious trouble without it. His king is much the weaker of the two, and his dark squares are leaky. The e5 square – the most important square on the whole board – is in Black's hands. And one more source of unfounded optimism for White in these kinds of positions is the illusion of an attack along the f-file against "the black king stranded in the center."

14...♘xh4 15.♕d3 ♘xg2 16.♔xg2 h4 17.♗f4 h3+ 18.♔h2 ♗xf4

18...♘f6 19.♗xe5 ♘g4+ 20.♔h1 ♘xe5–+.

19.♘xf4 ♘f6 20.♖ae1 ♘g4+ 21.♔h1 ♕b6 22.♕e2 f6 23.b3 ♗d7 24.♘d3 0-0-0 25.♘b5 ♗xb5 26.cxb5 ♘e5

Just a small inaccuracy. Simply 26...♖dg8 is better.

27.♘xe5 dxe5 28.a4 ♚b8 29.♕c4 h2 30.♖e2 ♖dg8 31. ♕d3 ♖g4 32.♖ff2 ♖hg8

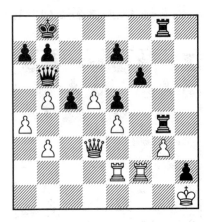

The difference lies in the two kings' respective degrees of safety. In major-piece endings, this is the paramount factor.

33.♖e3 ♕a5 34.♚xh2 ♕b4 35.♚g2 ♕d4 36.♕xd4 cxd4

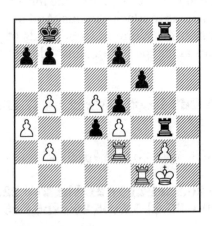

37.♖e1 ♖xg3+ 38.♚f1 ♖xb3

38...d3!!−+:

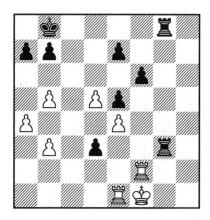

39.♖h2 ♖g1+ 40.♔f2 d2 41.♖xg1 ♖xg1 42.♔xg1 d1♕+.

The game concluded:

39.♖c1 ♖c3 40.♖fc2 ♖xc2 41.♖xc2 ♖g4 42.♖e2 d3 43.♖e3 d2 44.♔e2 ♖g2+ 45.♔d1 ♔c7 46.♖e2 ♖xe2 47.♔xe2 ♔b6 48.♔xd2 ♔a5 49.♔d3 ♔xa4 50.♔c4 b6 51.d6 exd6 52.♔d5 ♔xb5 53.♔xd6 a5 54.♔e6 a4 55.♔xf6 a3 56.♔xe5 a2 57.♔f6 a1♕+ 58.e5 ♔c6 59.♔e6 ♕d4 60.♔f5 ♔d5 61.♔g6 ♕xe5 62.♔f7 ♕d6 63.♔g8 ♕e7 64.♔h8 ♔e6 65.♔g8 ♔f6 66.♔h8 ♕g7# 0-1

35. Connyi (2555) – MASTER-GURU (2561)

1/5/2014

1.♘f3 d6 2.g3 c6 3.d4 ♘d7 4.♗g2 h6 5.0-0 g5 6.h3?!

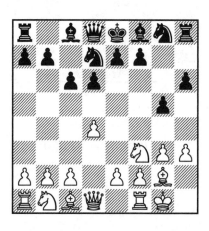

This is clearly not the product of necessity.

6...♘gf6 7.c4 g4!?

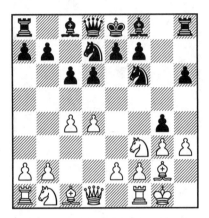

Right to the point! There is also a more restrained option: 7...
♗g7!? 8.♘c3 ♘f8 9.e4 g4 10.hxg4 ♘xg4 11.♘h4 ♕b6 12.♘f5 ♗xf5
13.exf5 ♕xd4:

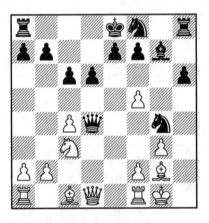

8.hxg4 ♘xg4 9.♘h4 h5 10.e4

(see diagram next page)

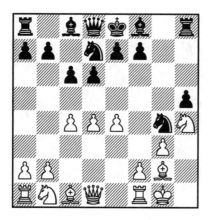

10...♕a5

10...♖g8!? is a worthy alternative: 11.♘c3 c5 12.dxc5 ♘xc5 13.♘f5 h4 14.♘xh4 ♘e5 15.♕c2 ♗g4 16.b3 e6 17.♗f4 ♘cd3 18.♗xe5 ♘xe5, attacking.

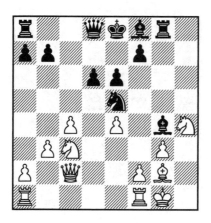

11.♘c3 ♗g7 12.a3 ♘f8 13.f3

(see diagram next page)

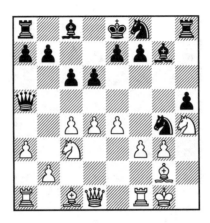

13...♛b6!?

Not one step backward (in the style of the early Tal). Another possibility is 13...c5!? 14.fxg4 ♝xd4+ 15.♔h2 hxg4 16.♘e2 ♝e5 17.♘f4 ♘g6 18.♘fxg6 fxg6 19.♔g1 ♝e6 with attack:

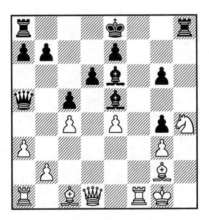

White's extra piece is little consolation for his predicament. A mere human being would generally find such a position impossible to hold.

14.fxg4 ♝xd4+ 15.♔h1 ♝xg4

15...♝xc3. This is now a standard idea. The following variation is not strictly forced, but it does illustrate Black's outstanding attacking possibilities: 16.bxc3 hxg4 17.♕e2 ♘g6 18.♗e3 ♘xh4 19.♗xb6 ♘f3+ 20.♗h3 ♖xh3+ 21.♕h2 ♖xh2#:

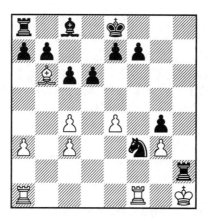

16.♕d3 ♘e6 17.♘a4 ♕c7 18.♘f5 ♗e5 19.♗f4 h4 20.♗xe5

20.♘xh4 ♘xf4 21.gxf4 ♖xh4+ 22.♔g1 ♗f6−+.

20...dxe5 21.♔h2?

21.♘xh4 is possible but doesn't save him: 21...♘d4 22.♘c3 0-0-0 23.♖xf7 ♘b3 24.♕f1 ♘xa1 25.♕xa1 ♗e6 26.♖f2 ♗xc4. White's insecure king decides everything.

21...hxg3+ 22.♔xg3 ♗xf5

22...♖g8! wins more quickly:

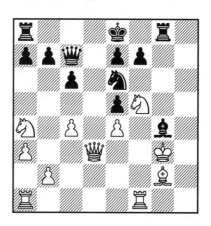

23.♔f2 ♗xf5 24.exf5 ♘f4 25.♕f3 e4 26.♕xe4 ♖xg2+ 27.♕xg2 ♘xg2 28.♔xg2 0-0-0−+.

23.♖xf5 ♘f4 24.♕f3 ♖g8+ 25.♔f2 ♖xg2+ 26.♔f1 0-0-0 27.♖xf4 ♖dg8 28.♕xg2 ♖xg2 29.♔xg2 exf4 30.♔f3 ♕d6 31.♖f1 ♕d3+ 32.♔g2 ♕xe4+ 33.♔g1 ♕d4+ 34.♔g2 ♕xc4 35.♘c3 e5 36.♖e1 f6 37.♔f3 ♕d3+ 38.♔g4 ♕g3+ 39.♔f5 f3 40.♔xf6 f2 41.♖f1 ♕g2 42.♖xf2 ♕xf2+ 43.♔e6 ♕xb2 44.♘e4 ♕xa3 45.♘d6+ ♕xd6+ 46.♔xd6 e4 0-1

36. Gin83 (2740) – Nemtsev_Igor (2718)

4/22/2015

1.c4 c6 2.b3 d6 3.♗b2 ♘d7 4.g3 ♘gf6

The "Castle" or "Lock" System.

5.♗g2 g5 6.e3 ♗g7 7.♘e2 h5

(see diagram next page)

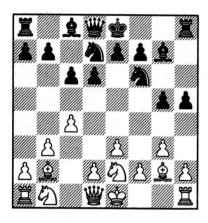

8.h4

8.0-0?! h4. In such cases, we are told to counter with an attack in the center. But there is no center.

The theme of Black's "centrally placed king" will still be a long time showing up.

9.d4 ♘f8 10.♘bc3 hxg3 11.hxg3 ♗h3 12.e4 ♕d7 13.e5 ♗xg2 14.♔xg2 ♕h3+ 15.♔f3 dxe5 16.d5 cxd5 17.♘xd5 ♘xd5 18.cxd5 e4+ 19.♔xe4 ♗xb2−+.

8...gxh4! 9.♖xh4 ♖g8

9...♘e5!? 10.♗xe5 dxe5 11.d4 exd4 12.exd4 ♗f5 13.♘bc3 ♕a5 14.♕d2 0-0-0.

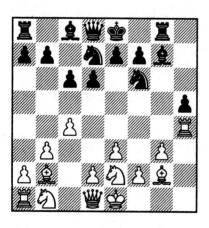

10.♘bc3 ♘e5 11.♘f4 ♗g4 12.♕c2 ♘f3+!

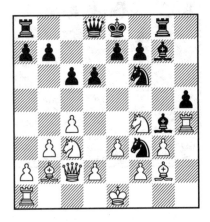

13.♗xf3 ♗xf3 14.♘h3 ♕a5 15.♖f4 ♗g4 16.♘g1 e5 17.♖xf6 ♗xf6 18.♘e4 ♗e7 19.f3 ♗e6 20.0-0-0 d5 21.♗c3 ♗b4 22.♘f6+ ♚e7 23.♘xg8+ ♖xg8 24.♗xb4+ ♕xb4 25.♘e2 dxc4 26.♕c3 ♕a3+

26...♕xc3+ 27.♘xc3 cxb3 28.axb3 ♖xg3–+.

27.♕b2 ♕b4 28.♕c3 a5 29.♕xb4+ axb4 30.♚b2 ♖d8 31.♘c1 c3+

31...e4!! 32.fxe4 (32.♘e2 exf3 33.♘d4 c3+ 34.dxc3 c5–+) 32...c3+ 33.♚c2 ♗g4 34.♖f1 cxd2–+.

32.♚c2 ♗f5+ 33.d3 ♗e6 34.e4 ♖h8 35.♘e2 h4 36.♖h1 h3 37.♖h2 f5 38.exf5 ♗xf5 39.g4 ♗g6 40.♘g3 ♖d8 41.♘e4 ♗xe4 42.fxe4 ♖h8 43.g5 ♚f7 0-1

37. Nikita_Selivanov (2782) – Nemtsev_Igor (2764)

4/22/2015

1.d4 d6 2.g3 c6 3.♗g2 ♘d7 4.c4 h6 5.♘f3 g5 6.0-0 ♗g7 7.♘c3 ♘f8 8.e4 ♘g6

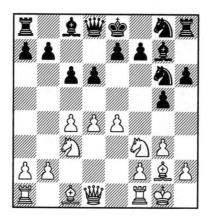

9.e5?!

Dubious – although the idea is fine in general: White needs to change the flow of events at any cost. But concretely, at this moment, the idea appears to be premature.

9...g4

9...dxe5!? at once is stronger. Here, the rule of thumb applies that we should immediately chop off the pawn that just advanced to e5, e.g. 9...dxe5:

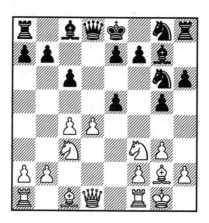

10.d5 (10.dxe5 ♕xd1 11.♖xd1 ♘xe5 12.♘xe5 ♗xe5 – simple: White is a pawn down with the worse position) 10...f5! 11.dxc6 bxc6:

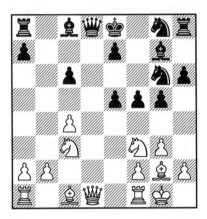

Don't forget that our c-pawn must stay put on c6 in order to protect against white pieces invading on b5 or d5.

12.♘d2 ♗d7 13.♕h5 ♔f7 14.♘b3 ♘f6 15.♕e2:

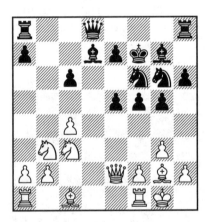

Here too, Black has two outstanding plans at his disposal:

1) 15...e4 16.f3 exf3 17.♕xf3 ♖b8 18.♔h1 h5 19.♗xg5 h4 20.gxh4 ♘xh4 21.♗xh4 ♖xh4 22.♕g3 ♖g4 23.♕f2 ♕c7 24.♗f3 ♖h8, and White cannot hold on;

2) 15...f4 16.♖d1 ♕c8 17.♘c5 ♗g4 18.f3 ♗f5 19.♘3e4 ♘xe4 20.♘xe4 ♗xe4 21.♕xe4 ♖d8 22.♖xd8 ♕xd8 23.♕e2 ♕d4+ 24.♔f1 ♖d8, and White faces death by strangulation.

10.♘h4

10.♘e1?! dxe5.

10...♘xh4 11.gxh4 dxe5 12.d5 cxd5

12...♗d7 is better and gives Black an advantage after 13.dxc6 bxc6 14.♕a4 ♕c7.

13.♘xd5 ♘f6 14.♕a4+ ♗d7 15.♕b4 ♖b8 16.♖d1 ♘xd5 17.♗xd5 ♕b6!?

Tremendous acrobatic maneuvering! This game was actually played by Elshad under my own login. I myself would not have considered this transition into the endgame. But nevertheless, it's very strong.

18.♕xb6 axb6 19.♗xf7+ ♔xf7 20.♖xd7 ♖hd8

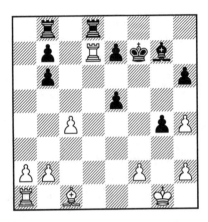

The undeveloped state of the white pieces is telling. This ending is fairly even.

21.♖xd8 ♖xd8 22.♗e3 e4 23.♖b1 ♖a8 24.a3 ♖a4 25.♗xb6 ♖xc4 26.♗e3 h5 27.♔g2 ♖c2 28.♖c1 ♖xb2 29.♖c7 ♔e6 30.♖c4 ♔f5 31.♖c5+ e5 32.♖c8 ♗f6 33.♖f8 ♔e6 34.a4

Simply blundering away a pawn. But all the same, the advantage has belonged to Black for a long time, and it is expressed in the fact that Black has what amounts to an extra piece – the king.

34...♗xh4 35.♖b8 ♗xf2 36.♗xf2 e3 37.a5 ♖xf2+ 38.♔g1 ♖xh2!

Very elegant!

39.♔xh2 e2 0-1

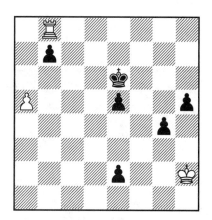

38.Atvaklinov (1995) – NemtsevIgor (1957)

Live Chess on Chess.com 4/26/2015

1.d3 d6 2.♘d2 c6 3.♘gf3 ♘d7 4.g3 h6 5.♗g2 g5 6.0-0 ♗g7 7.e4 ♘f8

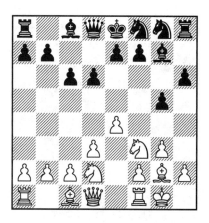

White is playing a King's Indian Attack.

8.c3 ♘g6 9.d4

White has expertly arranged his pawns in the center. His c-pawn should stand on c3, in order to support the d4-pawn.

9...g4!

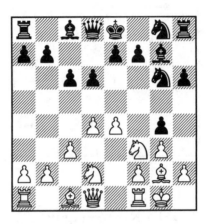

This is particularly timely – especially when our knight is on g6! For now, the white knight cannot go to h4.

10.♘e1 h5 11.f4?!

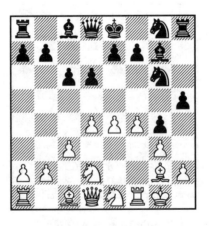

More than once, in this book, we have seen this kind of attempt at resolving a position. Now it would have been both correct and strong to play ...g4xf3. I wanted to see what would happen if Black did not capture the pawn *en passant*.

11...h4

11...gxf3! 12.♘exf3 h4 13.♘g5 ♗f6 14.♘c4 hxg3 15.hxg3 ♘h6. White's king is vulnerable; the e5 square is under my control! The initiative is clearly on Black's side. Even *Houdini* gives Black the upper hand.

12.f5 ♘f8 13.♖f2!?

Objectively, after 13.♕xg4!? ♖h7 14.♘d3 the advantage lies with White.

13...hxg3 14.hxg3 ♘f6 15.♘d3 ♘8h7 16.♘c4 b5 17.♘e3 ♘g5 18.e5 dxe5!

Even though Black's opening experiment has not been successful, the game itself taught us a lot – for example, that when White's e- or c-pawn crosses the demarcation line, it must be removed at once. Plus, of course, that in the opening one should capture *en passant* (11...gxf3!).

19.♞xe5?

With this single move, all of White's advantage goes away. He had to take with the pawn: 19.dxe5 ♞fe4 20.♖f4 ♞xg3 21.♖xg4 ♞h3+ 22.♗xh3 ♖xh3 23.♖xg7 ♖h1+ 24.♔g2 ♖xd1 25.♖g8+ ♔d7 26.♖xd8+ ♔xd8 27.♞xd1 ♞xf5 28.♗f4+−.

19...♞h3+ 20.♗xh3 ♖xh3 21.♔g2 ♞e4 22.♖f4 ♖xg3+ 23.♔f1 ♗xe5 24.♖xe4 ♖f3+ 25.♔e2 ♗f4 26.♞xg4 ♗xc1 27.♔xf3 ♗xb2 28.f6 ♛d5 29.♞f2 ♗xa1 30.♛xa1 ♗f5 31.♛e1 ♗xe4+ 32.♛xe4 ♛xe4+ 33.♞xe4 exf6 34.♞xf6+ ♔e7

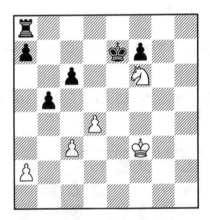

The endgame is absolutely hopeless for White; in the previous complications, as usual, he had some chances. It only remains for White to explain how completely he was winning, and how completely lost Black was.

35.♞e4 ♖h8 36.♞c5 ♖h2 37.a3 ♖a2 38.♞d3 ♖xa3 39.♞e5 ♖xc3+ 40.♔e4 b4 41.♞d3 b3 0-1

39.Atvaklinov (1978) − NemtsevIgor (1978)

Live Chess on Chess.com 4/26/2015

1.d3 d6 2.c4 c6 3.♞c3 ♞d7 4.g3 h6 5.♗g2 g5

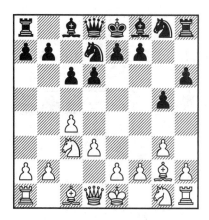

6.e4 ♗g7 7.♘ge2 ♘f8 8.h4 g4 9.♗e3 ♘e6 10.♕d2 h5 11.d4 ♕a5 12.d5 ♘f8 13.♘d4 c5 14.♘b3 ♕d8 15.0-0-0 ♘g6 16.♖he1 ♘e5 17.♕e2 a6 18.f4 gxf3 19.♗xf3 ♘f6 20.♘d2 ♘fg4 21.♗f4 b5 22.♔b1 ♕a5 23.♗g2 bxc4 24.♘xc4 ♕b4 25.♘xe5 ♘xe5 26.♕c2 ♘c4 27.♔a1 ♘xb2 28.♗d2 ♘c4 29.♖b1 ♕a5 30.♖b3 ♘xd2 31.♕xd2 c4 0-1

40. siso (2012) – NemtsevIgor (2212)

Live Chess on Chess.com /9/2015

1.d4 c6 2.c4 d6 3.♘c3 ♘d7 4.♘f3 h6 5.g3 g5 6.♗g2 ♗g7 7.0-0 ♘f8 8.e4

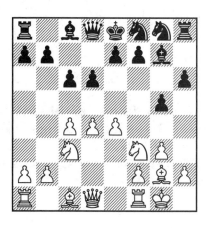

One of the *tabiyas* of the Elshad System.

8...g4 9.♘h4 ♗f6 10.♘f5 ♗xf5 11.exf5

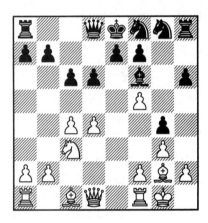

11...♕b6 12.♗e3 h5 13.♘e4 ♘d7 14.♕d2 ♕c7 15.♖ac1 h4

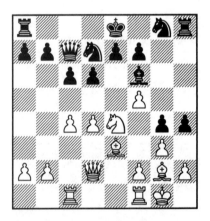

16.d5 c5 17.a3 ♘e5 18.b4 b6 19.♖fd1 ♖h5 20.♘xf6+ ♘xf6∓ 21.♗f4 ♖xf5 22.♖e1 hxg3 23.fxg3 ♘fd7 24.♗e4 ♖h5 25.♖f1 0-0-0 26.b5 ♖dh8 27.♖f2 f5 28.♗h1 ♕d8 29.a4 ♘f3+ 30.♗xf3 gxf3 31.♕e3 ♘f6 32.♕xf3 ♘g4 33.♖e2

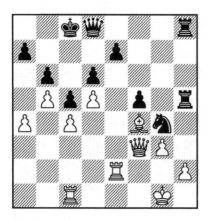

33...♖xh2

33...♘xh2! 34.♕d3 ♘g4–+.

34.♖xh2 ♖xh2 35.♖e1 ♕h8 36.♗xd6 ♕d4+ 37.♔f1 ♖f2+

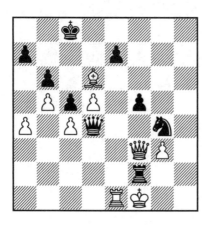

0-1

41. Vuhl – Elshad

2007

1.♘f3 c6 2.d4 d6 3.g3 h6 4.c4 ♘d7 5.♗g2 g5

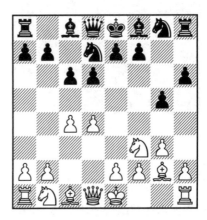

6.0-0 ♗g7 7.♘c3 ♘f8 8.e4 ♘g6!

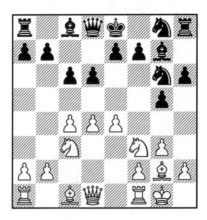

Another of this system's *tabiyas*. The knight is going right to g6, so that after an eventual ...g5-g4, the white knight won't be able to hop to h4.

White's main problem in this variation is that the rules tell him that he must deliver a blow in the center, when Black is attacking on the wing without fixing the center. But none of his breaks will work: on e4-e5 or c4-c5, Black simply takes that pawn off; and on d4-d5, he has ...c6-c5, closing up the center, switching the game to a positional track. But Black could also ignore White's play and continue with his own attack on White's king – the more so, that in that case (without ...c6-c5), Black's queen may pop out to b6, attacking the king along the a7-g1 diagonal.

9.♗e3?!

An inaccuracy. Arkady Vuhl is a grandmaster. Even so, a GM can sometimes lose his way when encountering an unfamiliar opening system. On e3, the bishop may now find itself in the (to us) now-familiar path of the black knight – ...♘g8-f6-g4!

9...♗e6

As we said before, ...♘f6-g4 is the strongest line here. The point is that once the g8-knight goes to f6, White will see that the jump to g4 is threatened and he will instinctively play h2-h3. And then, this gives Black a real target for ...g5-g4!.

10.b3

White is too cautious. He should have made up his mind to play 10.d5 ♗d7:

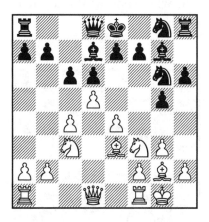

This is the whole idea behind Black's previous move: Black does not take on d5, but rather retreats to d7. Now the a1-h8 diagonal is opened up for the fianchettoed king's bishop on g7. But the most important point is that Black takes over the e5 square for his minor pieces. Black has several threats: ...g5-g4!, ...♛d8-b6!. (That last move is after we drive White's bishop away from e3, of course; this is why the bishop goes back to d7 rather than out to g4, which is reserved for either the pawn or the knight. On d7, the bishop protects the vitally important c6-pawn.)

11.♖c1 c5! 12.a3 ♘f6 13.h3?!:

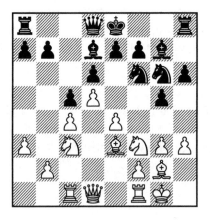

13...g4! 14.hxg4 ♘xg4 15.♗d2 h5 16.b4 cxb4 17.axb4 h4 18.♘xh4 ♘xh4 19.gxh4 ♗e5! 20.♖e1 ♖xh4 21.♛e2 a5 22.bxa5 ♛xa5. The attack encompasses the whole board; White can't hold everything.

10...♛a5!

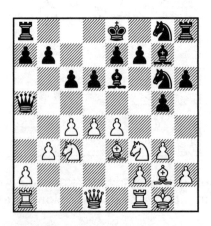

White Builds a Fortress with g2-g3 and ♗g2

One of this opening's principal maneuvers, not so much to attack the c3-knight as to prepare, if the occasion warrants, to slide the queen over to the kingside with ...♕a5-h5 after ...g5-g4 and the white knight goes away.

In this attacking plan, even the preparatory assault ...h5-h4! with the queen transfer to h5 can be good, as then the rook-and-queen battery starts to operate.

10...♘f6!?.

11.♖c1 g4 12.♘e1

12.♘d2 h5 13.e5 dxe5 14.d5 ♗d7 15.♘de4 ♖d8.

12...h5 13.f4?!

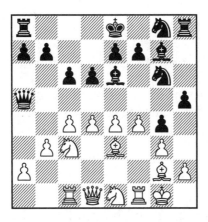

A strong player will find it very difficult psychologically to go on without any counterplay to embark on. So White overpresses. I advise you to remember this mistake by White, so typical in our opening. The king is much too exposed; but White suffers from the illusion that he is attacking the black king "stranded" in the center.

13...gxf3!

This is how it must be played! – the only proper choice in these kinds of positions. We must open up the dark squares around White's king.

14.♘xf3 ♗g4

It's a difficult matter, and almost impossible, to criticize this opening's author – a trailblazer, after all. But first 14...♘f6, keeping open the possibility of ...♘f6-g4, is stronger: 14...♘f6! 15.♗d2 h4 16.♘d5 ♛d8 17.♘xf6+ ♗xf6 18.♗g5 hxg3 19.hxg3 ♗g7, with the attack:

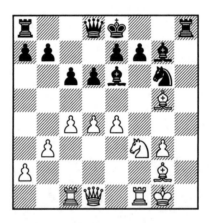

We keep the bishop, and later we move the queen to b6 and the rook to h5. After that, the king can even set up house on d7, clearing the h8 square for the other rook. White will struggle to avoid getting mated.

15.♛d2?!

The computer suggests h2-h3, but this is not something a human being would play.

15...♗xf3

15...h4! is even stronger, e.g. 15...h4! 16.♘xh4 ♘xh4 17.gxh4 ♛h5:

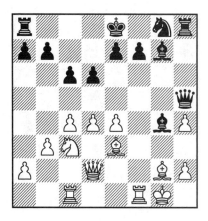

Completing the planned queen transfer to the kingside for his attack against the king. The difference in safety between the two kings is visible to the naked eye. And, as before, White lacks targets to shoot at.

16.♖xf3 h4 17.♖cf1 c5!?

Provocation! From a strategic viewpoint, this move is absolutely correct. He has to hit at the d4-pawn! But he has also given White an opportunity.

17...♘f6!?.

18.g4?!

18.♖xf7!? ♗f6 19.♖7xf6 ♘xf6 20.e5 cxd4 21.exf6 dxe3 22.♕xe3 hxg3 23.♕xg3 0-0-0 24.♕xg6 ♕xc3 25.♕f5+ ♔b8 26.f7 ♕d4+ 27.♖f2 ♕a1+ 28.♖f1 ♕d4+ 29.♖f2=; 18.e5! cxd4 19.♘d5 ♕xd2 20.♗xd2 ♘xe5 21.♘c7+ ♔d7 22.♘xa8 ♘xf3+ 23.♗xf3 hxg3 24.hxg3, and chances are dynamically equal in this complex endgame.

18...♗xd4! 19.♗xd4 cxd4 20.♕xd4 ♘e5!

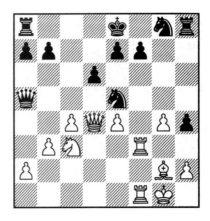

21.罝f5 h3!

Pay attention to this fairly typical attacking technique.

22.ዿf3 ᐁf6 23.g5 ᐁfd7 24.罝f4

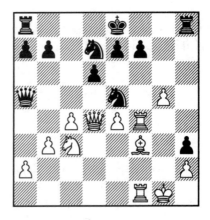

24...営b6

Going into an endgame is possible and interesting, but there was also a chance to continue his attack with the queens on, i.e. 24...罝g8!:

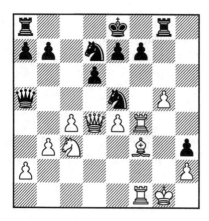

25.♖f5 e6 26.♖f4 ♘c6 27.♕e3 ♕xg5+ 28.♔h1 e5 29.♖g4 ♕xe3 30.♖xg8+ ♘f8 31.♘d5 ♕d3 32.♘f6+ ♔d8 33.♖xf8+ ♔e7 34.♖xa8 ♕xf1#.

Not strictly a forcing variation, but it does illustrate the proper handling of the attack in such positions.

25.♕xb6 axb6 26.a4 e6

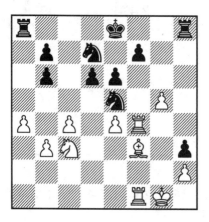

Black has a tremendous advantage in the endgame. The reason is that the white knight has neither support points in the center nor invasion squares – say, on d5. The black knight on e5 occupies a dominant position. Compare it, for example, to the bishop on f3. Besides, all of White's pawns in the center stand on light squares, making their own bishop bad.

27.♔f2

This is a blunder, but evidently White is exhausted from the preceding struggle: a typical psychological situation in the Elshad System.

27...♘d3+

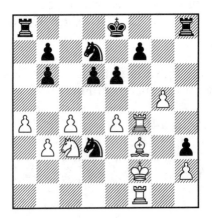

0-1

42. Veekley – Nemtsev I.

5/21/2015

1.g3 c6 2.♗g2 d6 3.d4 ♘d7 4.c3 h6 5.♘f3 g5 6.0-0 ♗g7 7.♘e1 g4!? 8.♘a3

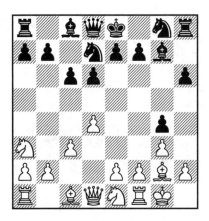

8...h5 9.♘d3

9.e4 ♘f8 10.♘c4 h4:

1) 11.♘d3 ♘g6 12.♕e2 ♗e6 13.♘e3 ♕a5 14.♘xg4 ♕h5 15.♗f3 ♕h7 16.♖e1 0-0-0 17.a4 hxg3 18.fxg3 ♘f6 19.♘xf6 ♗xf6 20.a5 ♖dg8;

2) 11.♘e3 ♘f6 12.♕e2 ♘g6 13.♘f5 ♗xf5 14.exf5 ♘f8 15.♘d3 ♖h5 16.♘f4 ♖xf5 17.♖e1 ♗h6 18.♕c2 ♕d7 19.a4 ♗xf4 20.♗xf4 hxg3 21.hxg3 ♖h5 22.a5 ♘e6 23.♗e3 a6 24.♖ad1 0-0-0 25.♕e2 d5! 26.b4 ♖dh8 27.♕c2 ♕c7∓;

3) 11.e5 dxe5 12.d5 cxd5 13.♗xd5 (13.♕xd5 ♕xd5 14.♗xd5 ♘f6 15.♗g2 e4∓) 13...♘e6 14.♕a4+ ♔f8 15.♗g2 e4 16.♗xe4 ♘c5 17.♕c2 ♗e6 18.♘e3 ♘xe4 19.♕xe4:

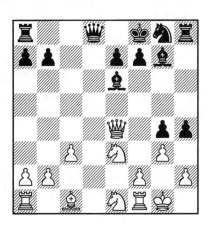

19...hxg3 (19...♕b6!? 20.♘1g2 ♘f6 21.♕c2 hxg3 22.hxg3 ♘d7! 23.♘h4 ♘e5 24.♘eg2 ♗f6 25.♗f4 ♘f3+ 26.♘xf3 gxf3 27.♘e3 ♕a5−+) 20.fxg3 ♕b6 (20...♘f6) 21.♘d3 ♘f6 22.♕b4 ♕xb4 23.♘xb4 ♖d8.

9...h4 10.♗g5

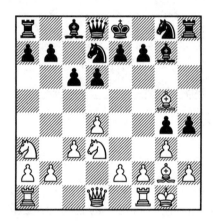

10...♘f8

10...♕a5!? 11.♗xh4 ♕h5 12.e4 ♗f6 13.f3.

10...hxg3! 11.hxg3 ♕a5 12.♗h4, and now:

1) 12...♕h5!? 13.♘f4 ♕h7 14.e4 ♗f6 15.♕xg4 ♘f8 16.♕f3 ♗xh4 17.gxh4 ♕xh4 18.♕g3 ♕h7!∓ 19.♖fe1 ♘e6 20.d5 ♘xf4 21.♕xf4 cxd5 22.exd5 ♗h3 23.♕e4 ♕h5 24.♘b5 ♗xg2 25.♕xg2 0-0-0 26.♖e3 f5;

2) 12...♘f8!? 13.♘c4 ♕b5 14.♕b3 (14.♘a3 ♕f5 15.♕a4 ♘g6 16.♗c6+ ♔f8!∓ 17.♗g2 ♘xh4 18.gxh4 ♕h5 19.♖fe1 ♕xh4 20.e3 g3 21.♔f1 ♗h3 22.♗xh3 ♕xh3+ 23.♔e2 ♕g4+ 24.♔d2 ♖h2 25.♕d1 gxf2 26.♕xg4 f1♕+ 27.♖e2 ♖xe2+ 28.♕xe2 ♕xa1−+) 14...♘g6 15.♕xb5 cxb5 16.♘e3 ♘xh4 17.gxh4 ♖xh4 18.♘d5 ♔d8 19.e4 e6 20.♘e3 ♔c7 21.f3 g3∓;

3) 12...♗f6 13.♗xf6 ♘gxf6 14.♖e1 ♕h5 15.♔f1 ♘f8 16.e4 ♘e6;

10...♗f6!? 11.♗xf6 ♘gxf6 12.e4 ♕a5 13.♖e1 ♕h5 14.e5 hxg3 15.hxg3 ♕h2+ 16.♔f1 dxe5 17.dxe5 ♘d5 18.♖e4 ♘f8 19.c4 ♗f5

20.cxd5 ♕xg2+ 21.♔xg2 ♗xe4+ 22.f3 ♗xf3+ (22...gxf3+ 23.♔f2 ♖h2+ 24.♔g1 ♖g2+ 25.♔f1 ♖h2) 23.♕xf3 gxf3+ 24.♔xf3 0-0-0−+.

11.♗xh4 ♘g6

11...♗h6!? 12.e4 (12.d5 c5! 13.e4 ♘g6 14.♖e1 f6 15.f3 ♘xh4 16.gxh4 gxf3 17.♕xf3 ♕b6 18.♘c4 ♕a6 19.b3 b5 20.♘e3 ♗xe3+ 21.♕xe3 ♘h6) 12...♘g6 13.e5 ♘xh4 14.gxh4 ♗g7 15.exd6 ♕xd6 16.♘c4 ♕h6 17.♖e1 ♕xh4 18.♘d6+ ♔f8 19.♘xc8 ♖xc8∓ 20.♕e2 ♕xh2+ 21.♔f1 ♖h4 22.d5 c5 23.♖ad1 ♕d6 24.c4 ♗d4 25.b4 cxb4 26.c5 ♗xc5 27.♘xc5 ♖xc5.

12.♗g5 ♕a5 13.d5

13.♗d2? ♕h5 14.h4 gxh3 15.♗f3 h2+ 16.♔h1 ♗g4 17.♗xg4 ♕xg4 18.♘c2 ♘f6 19.♘e3 ♕h3.

13...cxd5 14.♕b3 e6 15.♘b5 ♕b6 16.♗e3 ♕d8 17.♕b4 ♗f8 18.♘xa7 ♗d7 19.♕xb7 ♘f6 20.♗g5 ♗e7 21.♘c6 ♗xc6 22.♕xc6+ ♔f8 23.♕b7 ♖h5 24.♗e3 ♔g7 25.♗d4 ♕h8 26.♘f4

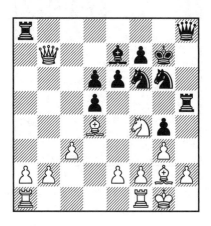

26...♘xf4

26...♖xh2!? 27.♘xg6 ♔xg6 28.♕xe7 ♖xg2+ 29.♔xg2 ♕h3+ 30.♔g1 e5 31.♕xd6 ♖h8 with mate to follow:

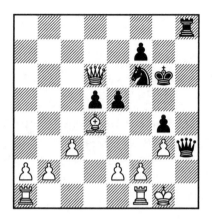

27.gxf4 ♖e8

27...e5! 28.fxe5 dxe5 29.♗b6 (29.♕xe7 exd4 30.cxd4 ♕b8!! *[30...
♖xh2 31.♗xd5]* 31.h3 gxh3 32.♗f3 ♖g5+ 33.♔h1 h2 34.♖ac1 ♕f4
35.♖c3 ♕f5 36.a3 ♕g6 37.♔xh2 ♖h8+):

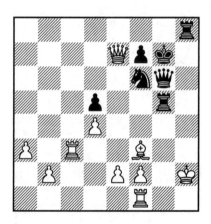

29...♖xh2 30.f3 g3 31.♖fd1 d4 32.cxd4 ♖xg2+ 33.♔xg2 ♕h2+
34.♔f1 ♕f2#.

28.f3 ♖xh2

28...gxf3 29.♖xf3 ♖xh2 30.♖g3+ ♔f8 31.♗xf6 ♗xf6 32.♖f1 ♕h4.

29.fxg4 e5 30.♗f2

30.fxe5 dxe5 31.♗xe5 ♗c5+ 32.♗d4 ♗xd4+ 33.cxd4 ♖xe2 34.♖f2 ♖xf2 35.♔xf2 ♕h4+ 36.♔f1 (36.♔g1 ♕g3) 36...♘xg4.

30...♘xg4 31.♗g3 ♖xg2+ 32.♔xg2 ♘e3+ 33.♔f2 ♘xf1 34.♖xf1 exf4 35.♗xf4 ♗h4+ 36.♗g3 ♕h5 37.♗xh4 ♕xe2+ 38.♔g3 ♖e3+ 39.♔f4 ♖e4+ 40.♔g5 ♕g4#

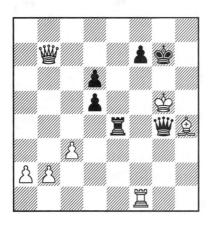

0-1

43. Jawschess1955 (2040) – NemtsevIgor (2077)

Live Chess on Chess.com 5/9/2015

1.c4 c6 2.♘c3 d6 3.d4 ♘d7 4.♘f3 h6 5.g3 g5

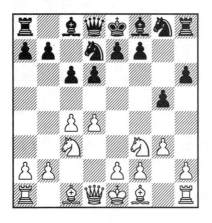

6.♗g2 ♗g7 7.e4 ♘f8 8.♗e3?!

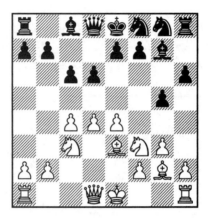

Once again, this bishop's development allows **Black to attack it** with tempo – maybe even to trade it off.

8...♘f6 9.♕c2 ♘g4 10.0-0-0

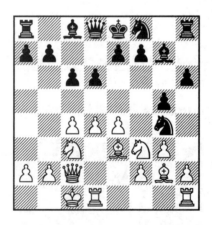

10.♗d2 (from a positional standpoint, this is always **superior**) 10...♘g6 11.h3 ♘f6 12.♗e3 g4! 13.hxg4 ♘xg4 14.♗d2 h5. The initiative belongs completely to Black, since castling queenside is for now impossible as then the f2-pawn would be lost.

10...♘xe3! 11.fxe3 g4

This is not a particularly good move here.

11...♗e6!?:

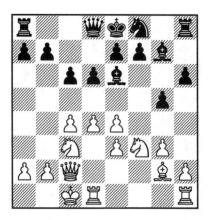

This is much better – we're provoking White into playing the d4-d5 advance! What good will that do? It will open up the diagonal for our bishop and make White's center pawns weak.

12.d5 cxd5! (99% of the time, we do not capture on d5 with this pawn, but here it is the strongest reply) 13.exd5 ♗g4 14.♔b1 ♖c8 15.♕d3 ♘d7 16.♖c1 ♗xf3 17.♗xf3 ♘e5 18.♕e2 ♖xc4, with great advantage to Black.

12.♘h4 ♗f6 13.♘f5 e6

13...♗xf5!? 14.exf5 ♕a5 15.e4 0-0-0 16.e5! dxe5 17.d5!. This idea for White leads to a struggle with roughly equal chances.

14.e5

14.♘xd6+ ♕xd6 15.e5 ♕d8 16.exf6 ♕xf6 17.d5 gives White a large plus.

14...exf5 15.exf6 ♕xf6 16.e4 f4 17.gxf4 ♕xf4+ 18.♔b1 ♘e6

18...♘g6! controls the e5 square.

19.d5 ♘c5 20.dxc6 bxc6 21.♕e2

21.e5? ♗xf5–+.

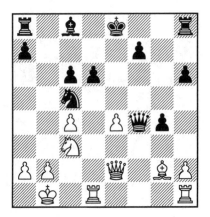

21...♕e5!

Look at that pawn on c6! That's the true hero of this whole battle! It prevents the white pieces from landing on the d5 square.

22.♖hf1 ♗e6 23.♕d2 ♔e7 24.♖f4 ♖ab8 25.♖df1 ♖b6!

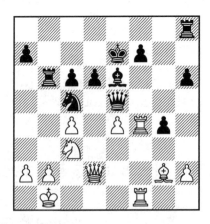

Paying White no attention, Black concentrates his forces for the attack on the opposing king.

26.♖1f2 ♖hb8 27.♘d1

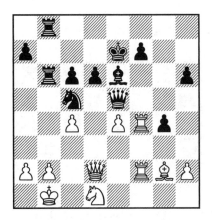

27...♗xc4 28.♖xg4 ♛e6 29.♖gf4

29.b3. This, too, fails to save him after 29...♗d3+ 30.♔c1 ♖xb3 31.axb3 ♘xb3+ 32.♔b2 ♘a5+ 33.♔c3 ♛c4#.

29...♗xa2+ 30.♔a1 ♘b3+ 31.♔xa2 ♘xd2+ 32.♔a1 ♖a6#

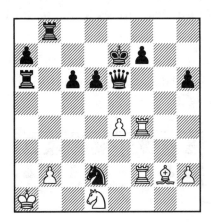

0-1

44. Kosarev – Elshad

Moscow 2012

1.♘f3 c6 2.g3 d6 3.♗g2 ♛a5 4.0-0 g5

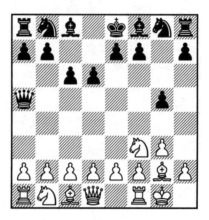

The highest success rate of for Black in Elshad's System is against the kingside fianchetto. Why is that? I tried playing White this way against Elshad, and not infrequently got mated in much the same way as you will see in this game. The problem is that the g3-pawn serves as a target for Black's attack with ...h7-h5-h4.

5.d3 g4! 6.♘e1

The other principled try is 6.♘h4, trying to blockade the kingside. There follows 6...♗g7!:

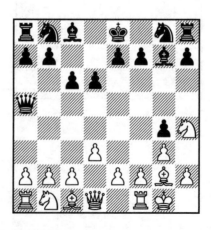

Black's main idea soon becomes clear: 7.♘c3 ♗f6!. Meanwhile, White has nothing constructive to do. Now, after 7...♗f6, White's kingside will get busted open. 8.e4 ♗xh4 9.gxh4 ♕h5 10.♗g5 f6 11.♗f4 ♘d7!. Another important maneuver. The knight follows the route ...b8-d7-f8-g6! so as to take the h4-pawn with the knight! 12.d4 (12.♘e2 ♘e5 13.♘g3 ♕xh4) 12...♘f8 13.♗g3 ♘g6 14.d5 ♗d7 15.♘e2 ♘xh4.

6...h5

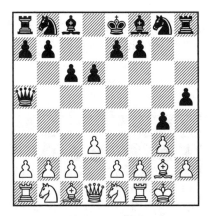

Already, *Houdini* shows a small plus for Black.

7.c4 h4 8.♘c3 ♕h5

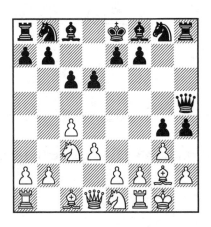

The main idea behind Black's whole setup! The queen has followed the a5-h5 route to the kingside, so the black rook turns out to be developed right on its original spot, without making a single move!

9.e4 ♗g7 10.♗e3 hxg3 11.fxg3

11.hxg3 ♕h2#.

11...♕xh2+ 12.♔f2 ♖h3 13.♖h1

13.♘e2 (the final line of defense) 13...♗xb2 14.♖h1 ♕xh1 15.♗xh1 ♗xa1 16.♕xa1 ♖xh1 17.♔g2 ♖h7.

13...♕xg3+

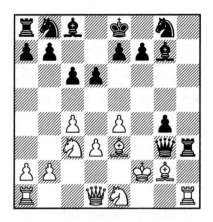

0-1

45. S. Tseitlin – Elshad

Moscow 2012

1.♘f3 c6 2.c4 ♕a5 3.g3 g5 4.♗g2 d6 5.0-0 g4 6.♘d4

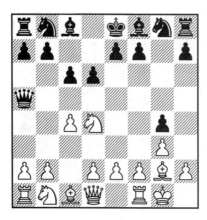

Previously, we have seen the knight move away to e1 or h4.

6...h5 7.d3 h4 8.e4 ♕h5

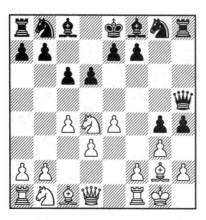

This diagram is not at all superfluous, showing off as it does Black's idea in all of its strategic splendor. The queen transfer is complete. Anyone who plays White against Elshad's System invariably falls into this trap.

9.♘c3 ♗g7 10.♘f5?

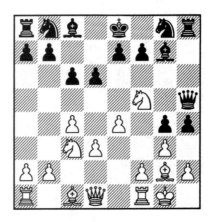

Another typical mistake by White. The knight that appears on f5 is eliminated at once. Now Black's attack becomes irresistible.

10...&xf5 11.exf5 hxg3!

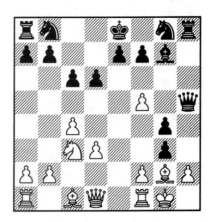

12.h3

12.fxg3 ♛xh2+ 13.♔f2 &d4+ 14.&e3 &xe3+ 15.♔xe3 ♛xg2 is hopeless for White.

12...gxf2+ 13.♖xf2

The alternative recapture 13.♔xf2 ♕xf5+ 14.♔g1 ♕g6! 15.♕xg4 ♕xg4 16.hxg4 ♗d4+ 17.♖f2 ♘f6 18.♗f3 ♘bd7 19.♘d1 ♗xf2+ 20.♘xf2 ♘e5 21.♔g2 ♖g8:

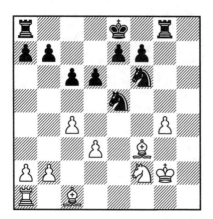

...is also rather sad for White.

13...♗d4 14.♕xg4 ♗xf2+ 15.♔xf2 ♘f6 16.♕xh5 ♖xh5 17.♗e3 ♘bd7 18.♖e1 ♘e5 19.♔e2 ♔d7!

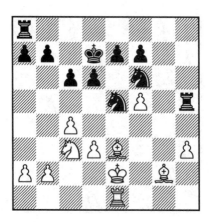

Typical – Elshad practically never castles. Now Black's last piece, which had lain dormant, comes to life.

20.b3 ♖g8 21.♗h1 ♖xh3 22.♗xa7 ♖h2+ 23.♗f2 ♖xf2+

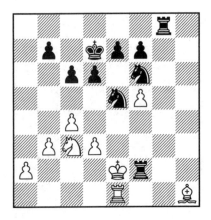

0-1

46. Averin – Elshad

1.♘f3 c6 2.g3 ♕a5 3.♗g2 g5 4.h3

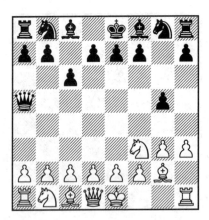

White has delayed, for a time, the ...g5-g4 advance by Black's pawn. But he still needs to realize he should not "castle into it."

4...h5 5.c3 ♗h6 6.0-0? g4! 7.♘h4 ♗g5

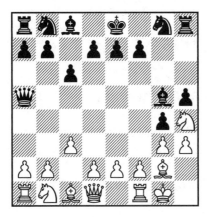

This was the idea behind developing the bishop to h6. Now White's kingside cannot avoid getting wrecked.

8.d4 ♗xh4 9.gxh4 d6 10.♔h2 gxh3 11.♗f3

11.♗xh3 is a bit better for White, but it's just too scary to play like this: 11...♗xh3 12.♔xh3 ♘f6 13.f3 ♘bd7 14.♖g1 0-0-0 15.e4 ♖dg8:

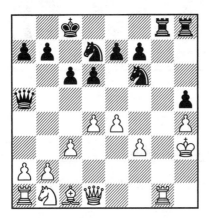

and Black continues with his massive kingside attack.

11...♘f6 12.e4 ♘g4+ 13.♗xg4 hxg4 14.♔g3?

So, where's the white king off to now?

14.♗g5 f6 15.♗f4 ♕h5 16.♗g3 ♘d7 17.♘d2 ♘f8 18.♕e1 ♘g6 19.f3 ♗e6 is bad, too.

14...♕h5 15.♗f4 ♘d7 16.♖g1 e5

16...♕xh4+ 17.♔h2 ♕xf2+ 18.♔h1 ♕xf4 would have been too prosaic for Elshad.

17.dxe5 dxe5 18.♗g5 f6 19.♗e3 h2 20.♖h1 ♕xh4+ 21.♔g2 ♕h3#

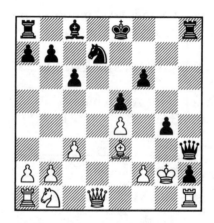

0-1

47. V. Nadezhdin – Elshad

1.c4 c6 2.♘f3 ♕a5 3.g3 g5 4.♗g2 d6

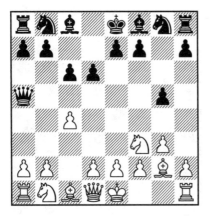

Valery Yurievich (playing White) is also a well-known "refuter" of the Elshad. A dedicated blitz player, he's always there at Sokolniki Park. He loves to simplify the game and knows how to make a hundred meaningless moves in a row without spoiling his position.

5.e3?!

Still, this move is inaccurate. White's combining e2-e3 with g2-g3 looks dubious.

5...♘d7

5...g4!?.

6.0-0 g4!

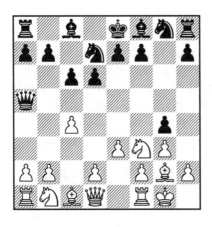

7.♘d4 ♞e5 8.d3 ♝g7 9.♘c3 h5

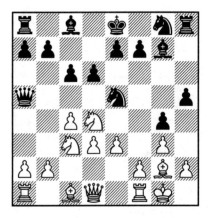

In Elshad's System, there exists a sort of optical illusion: at first, it looks as though White is playing by the book and setting up his pieces correctly; but then, a few moves later, there comes the realization that White has no defense. In this regard, let me relate a story Elshad once told me that he heard from IM Maksim Notkin, editor-in-chief of *64 – Chess Review*. (I contacted Maksim on Facebook; he confirmed that this had actually happened and told me that he could verify the details with Alexander Morozevich. I had not expected this degree of confirmation!)

This is a pretty funny story: in Dagomys, during the Russian Team Championship, Morozevich was in a restaurant, sharing his impressions of some blitz games he had played at the TsDSh *[Central House of Chess – Tr.]* with somebody named "Elshad." The gist of what he was saying was that he was playing this "Elshad," making one "best" move after the other; and yet he could see that his position was getting worse, move by move. At one point, his position was dead lost – even though Alexander had been playing only the "right" moves. Elshad lost that game after a terrible blunder. But that impression, made on a very strong grandmaster who has never, ever been known for dull play – that means a lot.

10.♘b3 ♛c7 11.♛e2 a5 12.a4 ♞f6 13.♝d2 ♛b6 14.♖a3

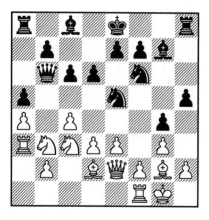

I'm just going to say it: White has placed his pieces awkwardly.

14...h4 15.d4 ♘f3+! 16.♗xf3 gxf3 17.♕xf3 ♗g4 18.♕g2

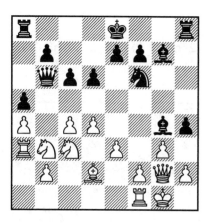

The decisive moment! Here Elshad played – as usual – something truly original!

18...h3

18...hxg3:

(see diagram next page)

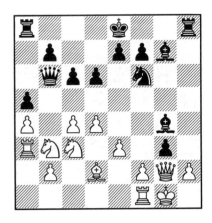

Opening the position this way would have been very strong!

19.fxg3 ♗h3 20.♕f3 ♗xf1 21.♕xf1 ♕c7 22.♕f3 ♕d7, initiating the second wave of the attack on White's king by transferring the queen to h3!

19.♕h1 ♕a6 20.♖c1 ♕xc4 21.♘b5 ♕d3 22.♘c7+ ♔f8 23.♘xa8

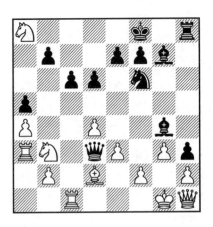

White is a whole rook up – and yet *Houdini* says he has zero advantage!

23...♗h6 24.f4? ♗xf4

Here 24...♘e4!:

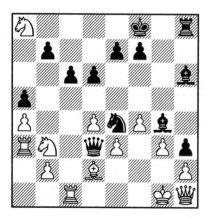

wins right away, for example 25.♖e1 ♘xd2 26.♘xd2 ♕xd2 27.♖aa1
♗e2 28.♔f2 ♗g4+ 29.♔g1 d5 30.♔f1 ♕d3+ 31.♔f2 ♔g7 32.♘b6 ♕b3
33.♕f1 (letting his queen out, but it's too late) 33...♕xb6−+.

**25.exf4 ♘e4 26.♖e1 ♘xg3 27.hxg3 ♕xg3+ 28.♔f1 ♗f3
29.♘c5**

29.♘c1 ♗g2+ 30.♔e2 ♕g4+ 31.♔f2 ♗xh1 32.♖g3 ♕c8 33.♖xh1
♕xa8 34.♖hxh3 ♖xh3 35.♖xh3 ♕a6.

29...♗g2+ 30.♔e2 ♕g4+ 31.♔e3 ♕f3#

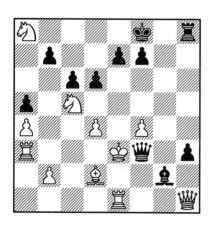

Checkmates like this are a real tribute to those who seek new and unusual pathways in chess!

0-1

48. Y. Kurlakov– Elshad

1.c4 c6 2.♘c3 ♛a5 3.g3 h6 4.♘f3 g5 5.♗g2 ♗g7 6.0-0

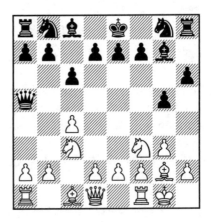

It would be interesting to play ...g5-g4; where would White's knight go then?

6...d6

6...g4!? 7.♘h4 ♗f6 8.d4 ♗xh4 9.gxh4 d6. The white king's cottage is in ruins; not everybody wants to play with his king like this.

7.♛c2 ♘d7

7...g4!?.

8.b3 ♘f8 9.♗b2 ♘g6 10.d4

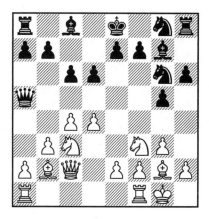

10...g4!

This is why the black knight undertook that long trek to g6: now the white knight would not have a good spot to retreat to.

11.♘e1 h5!?

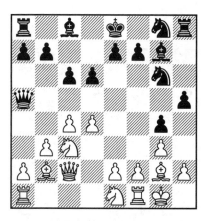

In the Elshad System, this is a move with a definite idea: Black prepares to play ...h5-h4, followed by putting his queen on h5. Nonetheless, right now he could (and should) take the d4-pawn: 11...♗xd4 12.♖d1 ♗g7 13.♘d3 ♘f6.

12.罝d1?!

An inaccuracy. But of course, one needs to be aware of Black's main idea in this position (moving the queen to h5) in order to prevent it. For this purpose, White had at his disposal two moves:

1) 12.d5!? c5 13.分d3 h4 14.a3 豐d8 15.b4 b6 16.分e4 空f8 17.鿨xg7+ 空xg7, and chances are equal in the coming battle. It won't be easy for Black to bring his queen into the attack on White's kingside.

2) 12.c5!? dxc5! 13.dxc5 h4 (13...豐xc5? 14.分d3 豐f5 15.鿨e4 豐g5 16.鿨xc6+! 空f8; 16...bxc6? 17.分e4 豐h6 18.鿨xg7 豐xg7 19.豐xc6+ 空f8 20.豐xa8+−) 14.分e4 空f8 15.鿨xg7+ 空xg7 16.分d3 f5, with very complex play. Chances are equal.

12...h4 13.e3?

A mistake. This was his last chance to keep the black queen from shooting over to the kingside.

13...豐h5

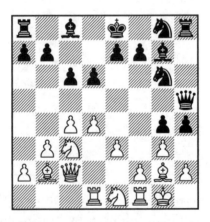

14.鿨h1 分f6 15.分d3 鿨f5 16.e4 鿨d7 17.豐e2 空f8

Here it is preferable to castle queenside anyway – if only to get the other rook into the attack.

18.e5 ♘e8 19.♖fe1 hxg3 20.fxg3 dxe5 21.dxe5 ♘c7 22.♘c5 ♗f5 23.♘xb7?

Greedy.

23...♘e6 24.♖f1 ♗h6 25.♘e4 ♗e3+

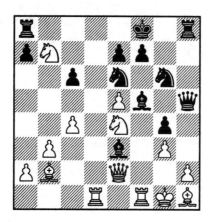

Mate in two is unavoidable.

26.♖f2 ♕xh2+ 27.♔f1 ♕xh1# 0-1

49. N. Molchanov – Elshad

1.c4 c6 2.g3 ♕a5 3.♘c3 g5

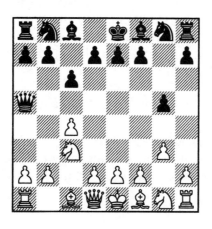

This is the move that defines the "face" of the Elshad System. Of course, we could also begin with 3...h6, not "alarming" White for now.

4.♗g2 ♗g7 5.d4 d6 6.e4 ♘d7 7.♗e3 ♘f8 8.♕d2

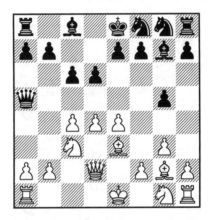

8...g4

The principled decision! Alternatively, he could have played in a more restrained manner with 8...h6.

9.h4 gxh3!?

And there it is! On the one hand, the g4-pawn is a wedge, preventing White's kingside from developing normally; on the other hand, here we have yet another sharp idea – a clear possibility for creative growth, a position so unusual that an unprepared opponent (and how could there be a "prepared opponent" here?) would lose the thread of the game.

10.♘xh3 ♗e6 11.b3 ♘f6 12.♘f4 ♘g4 13.♘xe6?!

This move is mistaken, because the whole Elshad System is based around a dark-square strategy, and now the black knight starts exerting pressure on d4 from e6. That is Black's chief aim here.

13...♘xe6 14.♗h3 ♘xe3 15.♗xe6 fxe6

Simple and strong. Black also has another tactical possibility:
15...♘c2+!? 16.♕xc2 ♗xd4 17.♗xf7+ ♔xf7 18.♖c1 ♖af8 19.♔f1 ♔e8.

16.fxe3

16.♕xe3? c5 is just bad for White.

16...♕g5 17.0-0-0 h5 18.♖df1 ♔d7 19.e5 ♗h6 20.♖f3

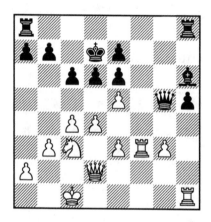

20...♖af8! 21.♖hf1 ♖xf3 22.♖xf3 ♕g4 23.♕f2 d5?

23...♕xd4 24.♔b2 ♕e5 wins immediately.

24.♔d2 ♖g8 25.cxd5 cxd5 26.♘a4 b6 27.♕e2 ♕xd4+ 0-1

50. B. Krasavtsev – Elshad

**1.e4 d6 2.d4 ♘d7 3.♘c3 h6 4.g3 c6 5.♗g2 g5 6.♘ge2 ♗g7
7.♗e3 ♕a5 8.♕d2 b5 9.h4 ♖b8 10.f4 ♘b6 11.b3 ♗g4 12.hxg5
hxg5 13.♖xh8 ♗xh8 14.fxg5 c5 15.a4 b4 16.♘d5 ♘xd5
17.exd5 c4 18.bxc4 ♖c8 19.c5 dxc5 20.♖d1 c4 21.♗f4 c3
22.♕e3 b3 23.cxb3 c2+ 24.♖d2 ♗xe2 0-1**

Chapter 3

Classical Variation: White Plays ♘f3, ♗e2, and 0-0

51. Klyuka_Sergey (2713) – Nemtsev_Igor (2761)

1/17/2015

1.d4 c6 2.♘f3 d6 3.c4 ♛a5+

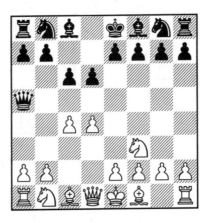

In the early stages of this variation's development, Elshad would often play this way. The check is not nearly as pointless as it might appear at first. Black's idea is that if a white piece interposes on d2, then it will act as an obstacle on this key square, hindering the development of other pieces. Most importantly, it severs the connection between the queen and the d4-pawn. Black's other idea is that from a5, the queen could eventually go to h5, with mate threats against the white king.

4.♘c3 h6 5.e4 g5

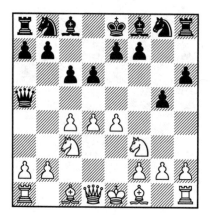

The starting point for this variation.

6.h3

All quite logical. We should not underestimate the threat of ...g5-g4!

6...♗g7 7.♗e3 ♘d7 8.♗e2 ♘f8 9.0-0

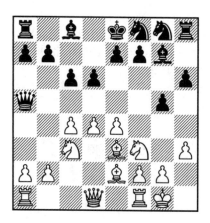

9...♘e6

Chapter 3

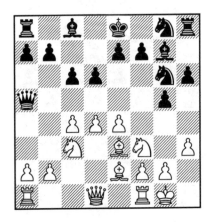

But here 9...♘g6! is even better. The point is that we can launch our attack on the white king at once with ...g5-g4!, meaning that we'll need to have our pieces closer to the kingside, for example (9...♘g6) 10.a3 ♘f6 11.b4 ♕c7 12.♖c1 g4! 13.hxg4 ♘g4 14.♕d2 h5 15.♖cd1 ♘xe3 16.♕xe3 ♗h6 17.♕d3 ♖g8 18.♕c2 ♘f4 19.♘e1 ♗h3, and White cannot hold.

10.a3 ♘f6 11.b4 ♕c7 12.♖c1 g4! 13.hxg4 ♘xg4 14.♗f4?? h5??

Yes, White hung the bishop; and yes, Black could have grabbed it. But still – I give this game as an example of a standard attack on the king in this opening.

15.♗g3 ♖g8

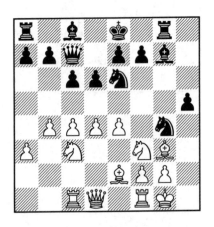

In the Elshad, the rook often lays siege along the g-file – grinning at White's king from afar.

16.♘h4 ♘xd4

It's easier than anything to lose the thread in an unusual setup! White just lost sight of the board!

17.f3 ♘e3 18.♕d2 ♘xf1 19.♗xf1 ♘b3 20.♕g5 ♘xc1

0-1

52. Semyonov_Rinat (2423) – Nemtsev_Igor (2722)

3/23/2015

1.d4 c6 2.c4 d6 3.♘f3 ♘d7 4.♘c3 h6 5.e4 g5 6.♗d3

My opponent is an international master. All the more interesting, then, to follow the progress of the game.

6...♗g7 7.0-0 ♘f8

7...g4!. Once White breaks the connection between the queen and the d4-pawn, it's time to go after the pawn. 8.♘h4 ♗xd4 9.♕xg4 ♘gf6 10.♕d1 ♘e5 11.♘f5 ♗xc3 12.bxc3 ♖g8:

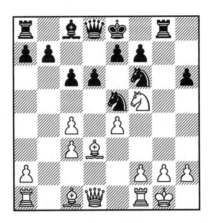

8.♗e3 ♘e6

8...♘f6!? is better. The threat of jumping to g4 induces White to play h2-h3, which we need as a target to latch onto in our kingside attack: 9.h3 g4 10.hxg4 ♘xg4 11.♗d2 ♘e6 12.♗e2 ♖g8! 13.d5 ♘d4 14.♘xd4 ♗xd4 15.♗xg4 ♗xg4 16.♕b3 ♗f3:

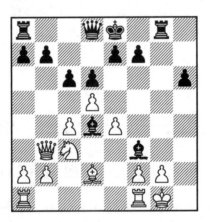

And the game is over.

9.d5 ♘f8 10.♘d4 c5 11.♘f5 ♗xf5 12.exf5 ♘d7!

Black must control the e5 square at all times!

13.f4 ♘gf6

13...gxf4!? 14.♗xf4 ♗d4+ (14...♗e5 15.♘e4 ♘gf6 16.♘xf6+ exf6) 15.♔h1 ♘e5 16.♘e2 ♘f6 17.♘xd4 cxd4 18.♗xe5 dxe5 19.♕e2 ♕d6 20.♖ae1 ♘d7.

14.fxg5

14.g3 ♕b6 15.♕e2 0-0-0 16.♖ab1 h5 17.fxg5 ♘g4 18.♔g2 ♘xe3+ 19.♕xe3 ♗d4 20.♕d2 ♘e5 (20...h4 21.♘e2 hxg3 22.hxg3) 21.h4.

14...hxg5 15.♗xg5 ♘e5

15...♕b6!?.

16.♗f4 ♘h5 17.♗e3 ♕b6 18.♖b1 ♘f6 19.♗e2 0-0-0 20.a3 ♗h6 21.♗f2 ♖dg8 22.b4

22...♕c7

22...♘eg4!? 23.bxc5 ♗f4!! 24.cxb6 ♗xh2+ 25.♔h1 ♗g3+ 26.♔g1=.

23.♘b5 ♕b8 24.bxc5 dxc5 25.♗g3

25.d6 a6 26.♘c7 ♗f4.

25...♗e3+ 26.♖f2 ♖xg3 27.hxg3 ♘e4

White could not handle the tactical complications. On certain moves, White did have opportunities to achieve a positive result; but exploiting them is very difficult when you don't understand what's going on at the board.

28.♗h5 ♗xf2+ 29.♔f1 ♖xh5! 30.♕xh5 ♘xg3+ 0-1

53. moor777 (2718) – Nemtsev_Igor (2781)

1/21/2015

1.d4 c6 2.c4 ♕a5+ 3.♘c3 d6 4.♘f3 h6 5.e4 g5

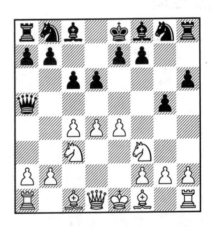

6.h3

One possible move – and not a bad one, either. White correctly defends against ...g5-g4.

6...♗g7 7.♗e2 ♘d7 8.0-0 ♘f8 9.♗e3

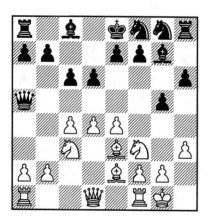

An important crossroads. Black can now bring his knight to g6 in order to mount an immediate assault on the white king, which has imprudently castled!

9...♘e6

9...♘g6!? 10.♖c1 ♘f6 11.a3 g4!:

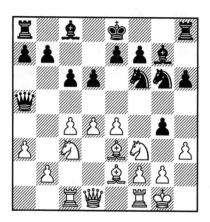

Standing at g6, the knight, in some lines, deters White's knight from going to h4.

12.hxg4 ♘xg4 13.♗d2 ♕h5!:

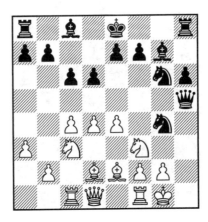

A very important transfer of the queen, preparing for the attack on the king! (By the way, the queen moved out to a5 at the start of the game mainly in order to make this maneuver!)

14.♖e1 ♗xd4, and that's all she wrote for White.

10.♘h2 ♘f6

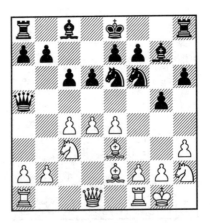

The magic of this position lies in the fact that White, naturally, wants to smash through Black's position in the center! But how? On e4-e5, we just take the e-pawn. On d4-d5, we retreat the knight to f8 and then take over the e5 square with ...♘f8-g6-e5; while if c4-c5, we have to take on c5. In other words, Black *does not* allow White to take on d6. Not under any circumstances!

11.d5 ♘f8 12.♘g4 ♘xg4

12...♘6d7 13.♗d4 ♗xd4 14.♕xd4 f6:

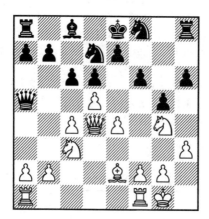

Have you seen this a lot on the chessboard? I can only recall a game Korchnoi–Karpov from the Alekhine Memorial, held in Moscow in 1971, in which Karpov traded off his dark-squared bishop in a similar (well, relatively similar) situation, and then went ...f7-f6.

12...♗xg4 13.♗xg4 ♘g6.

13.♗xg4 c5 14.f4?!

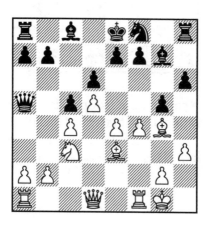

Reminds me of my game with Naumkin: in principle, the same mistake.

14...♛b4 15.♕d2 ♕xc4 16.fxg5 ♝xg4 17.hxg4 ♞g6

17...hxg5! 18.♝xg5 (18.♕f2 ♝f6 19.♖ac1 ♞g6 20.♖c2 ♞e5 21.♕f5 ♕d3 22.♖e2 ♞c4−+) 18...♞g6 19.♖ac1 ♞e5 20.♖ce1 ♞xg4−+.

18.gxh6 ♝d4 19.♝xd4 cxd4 20.♞e2 d3 21.♞g3 ♞e5 22.♖ae1 ♕d4+ 23.♔h1 ♞xg4 24.♕g5 ♖xh6+ 25.♞h5 ♞f2+ 26.♖xf2 ♕xf2 27.♖d1 ♖g6 0-1

54. stammargg (2822) – Nemtsev_Igor (2729)

4/22/2015

1.c4 c6 2.d4 h6

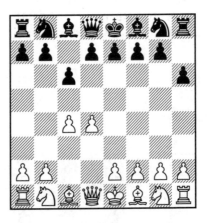

This game has a curious prehistory. Elshad once dropped in on me for the transcription of an interview I had done with him for this book. Here, after an interesting conversation, we decided to play a bit on Chess Planet. This is the game Elshad played. I noticed a few new ideas, and I will share them here. Generally speaking, it is incredibly interesting to talk to somebody who sees doors where most of us see only walls.

3.♘f3 g5 4.h3

A very natural and understandable reaction , so that the...g5-g4 advance doesn't keep hanging over him. But White doesn't realize that, on h3, the pawn will now become the hook for our attack on his king.

4...♗g7 5.e4 d6 6.♘c3 ♘d7 7.♗e3

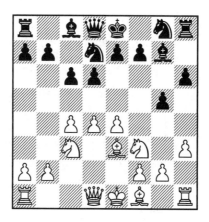

7...a5!?

And here it is – the fresh idea! Where's the pawn going, and why? It's clearing a path for the rook!

8.♗d3 a4 9.♘xa4

Why not take it? If you don't, it will keep going to a3!

9...♘f8 10.♘c3 ♘g6 11.♕d2 ♕a5 12.0-0

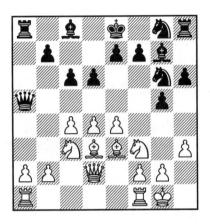

12...g4!

The black a-pawn, which gave itself up so that the rook and queen could become active, was not such a great price to pay for the attack that Black now unleashes.

13.hxg4 ♗xg4

Also strong is 13...♘f6, with the idea of taking on g4 with the knight: 14.♘h2 h5 15.g5 ♗g4 16.♘xg4 hxg4. This opens the h-file, with a powerful attack looming.

14.♘h2 ♘f6 15.b4 ♕h5

Not letting himself get distracted by White's b-pawn. Here it's important to understand that, in Elshad's System, the winner is the one who finds his way better in the positions that arise. No one should be led astray by the fact that engines unfailingly show +1.50, for we play against humans, not machines.

16.f3 ♗d7 17.g4 ♕h3! 18.♕g2 ♕xg2+ 19.♔xg2 ♖a3

And by now, even *Komodo* understands (if "understands" is the right word for a computer program): -1.50.

20.♖ac1 h5 21.g5 ♘g8

And here, Black has a devastating resource – which, by the way, Elshad pointed out immediately after the game: 21...♘g4!! 22.fxg4 hxg4 23.♖fd1 ♖h3 24.♘f1 ♘h4+ 25.♔g1 ♖xe3 26.♘xe3 ♗xd4 27.♔f2 ♗xc3. Very nice! The white pieces, laid out across the third rank like pieces of meat on a skewer, get gobbled up most unnaturally.

22.f4 e5 23.dxe5 dxe5 24.f5 ♘f4+ 25.♗xf4 exf4 26.f6 ♘xf6! 27.gxf6 ♗xf6 28.e5 ♗xe5 29.♖fe1 f6 30.♘f3 ♖g8+ 31.♔f2 ♖g3 32.♘xe5 fxe5 33.♖xe5+ ♔d8 34.♔e2 ♗g4+ 35.♔d2 ♖g2+ 36.♔e1 f3 37.♗f1 ♖b2 38.♘d1 ♖xb4

38...f2+ 39.♘xf2 ♖axa2 40.♘xg4 hxg4 41.♖d1+ ♔c7 42.c5 ♔b8 43.♖e8+ ♔a7 44.♖e7 ♖b3 45.b5 ♖xb5 46.♗xb5 cxb5 47.c6 ♖c2 48.♖xb7+.

39.c5 ♖xa2 40.♘c3 f2#

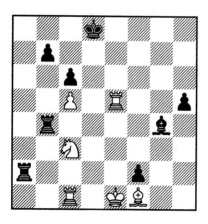

Exhausted by a long and difficult defense, White misses mate.

0-1

55. EvgenyAtarov (2122) – NemtsevIgor (2167)

Live Chess on Chess.com 6/10/2015

1.d4 c6 2.e4 d6 3.c4 ♘d7 4.♘c3 h6 5.♘f3 g5 6.h3 ♗g7 7.♗e2 ♘f8 8.♗e3 ♘e6 9.♕d2 ♕a5 10.0-0 ♘f6 11.♖ab1

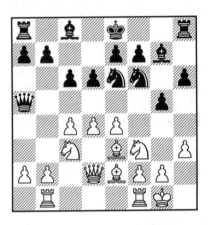

White wishes to attack in the center and on the queen's wing; this would be correct strategy. But Black also has a clear plan, involving an attack on the white king. Although White won this game, we will show many interesting possibilities for Black that were not exploited in this contest.

11...g4!

A standard shot in Elshad's System. The h3-pawn is a target and Black finds a way to exploit it. White doesn't have much of a choice.

12.hxg4

Any retreat by the knight is met by 12...gxh3, with the complete destruction of White's castled position.

12...♘xg4 13.♗f4

If Black is allowed to take this bishop with a knight, then the super-bishop on g7 will be left unopposed and all of White's kingside dark squares will belong to it. This is the Elshad System's dark-square strategy.

13...♘xf4 14.♕xf4

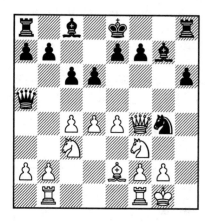

14...h5

14...♕h5!. This was the main idea behind bringing the queen out to a5 – transferring it to h5 for an attack on the king. Let's see: 15.♖bd1 ♖g8! 16.♖fe1 ♗f6 17.♘h2 ♗xd4! 18.♖xd4 e5 19.♗xg4 ♗xg4 20.♘xg4 ♖xg4 21.♕f6 ♖h4 22.f3 exd4 23.♕xd4 ♖h1+ 24.♔f2 ♕h4+ 25.g3 ♖h2+ 26.♔e3 ♕g5+ 27.♔d3 ♖d2#:

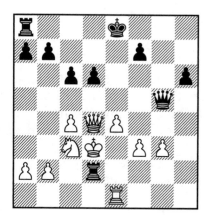

15.♘g5?!

Looks terrifying, but actually a mistake. The problem is that in the Elshad System White generally doesn't threaten to take on f7, as the black king has a nice little trail to follow: ...♚e8-d8-c7. But now the d4-pawn is left unprotected, and it must be captured.

15...f6

15...♗xd4! 16.♕xf7+ ♚d8 17.♘e6+ (17.♗xg4 ♕xg5 18.♗xc8 ♖xc8 19.♘e2 ♖g8 20.g3 ♗b6 21.♕f5 ♕g4 22.♕xg4 ♖xg4∓; 17.♕f4 ♖g8 18.♘f3 ♗xc3 19.bxc3 ♕xc3 20.♖fd1 ♕g7∓) 17...♗xe6 18.♕xe6 ♕g5 19.♕f5 ♕h4 20.♕f4 ♗e5:

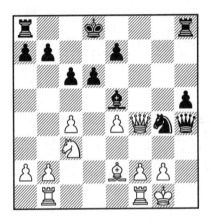

16.♘f3 ♗h6?!

A very important moment. I had to bring my queen into the attack; fortunately, a method for doing that existed: ...h5-h4!!, followed by shifting the queen over to h5. Let's see: 16...h4! 17.b4 ♕h5, and now 18.♘h2, attempting to trade off Black's attacking forces. The problem is that, even in the endgame, Black stands better: 18.♕d2 (with the queens off, Black's attack slices through like a knife through butter) 18...h3 19.g3 ♗h6 20.♕d1 h2+ 21.♚h1 ♕h3 22.♕d3 ♘e3 23.fxe3 ♕xg3 (threatening mate with ...♗h3)

24.♗d1 ♗h3 25.♕e2 ♗xf1 26.♕xf1 ♗xe3 27.♕g2 ♕xg2+ 28.♔xg2 h1♕+ 29.♔g3 ♕h3#:

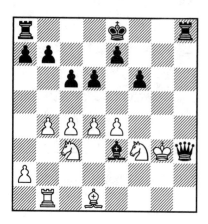

After 18.♘h2, play might continue 18...♗h6 19.♕f3 (19.♗xg4 ♗xf4 20.♗xh5+ ♖xh5 21.♘f3 ♔f7 22.b5 h3 23.g3 ♗h6 24.♔h2 ♗g4∓) 19... ♖g8 20.♕h3 ♕g5 21.♗xg4 ♗xg4 22.♘xg4 ♕xg4 23.♕xg4 ♖xg4 24.f3 ♗e3+ 25.♔h1 ♖g6 26.d5 ♖c8 27.dxc6 ♖xc6, with a clear advantage for Black in the ending.

17.♕g3 ♗d7 18.b4 ♕c7 19.b5 ♕a5 20.♖b3 ♔f7 21.e5

Otherwise Black simply slides his currently out-of-play rook over to the kingside, with an unstoppable attack. Therefore, White strikes in the center.

21...dxe5

21...h4! deserves attention. The idea behind this pawn sacrifice is plain as day – to open lines for the attack, e.g. 21...h4 22.♘xh4 ♖ag8 23.exd6 ♗d2 24.dxe7 ♘e5 25.e8♕+ ♗xe8 26.♕h3 ♗d7 27.♕h2 ♗xc3 28.dxe5 ♗xe5 29.g3. Not a strictly forcing variation, but it does show White's typical problems here.

22.dxe5 ♖ag8 23.exf6 ♘xf6 24.♕e5

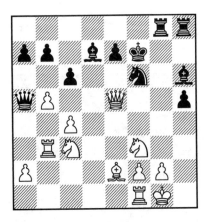

The culmination of the struggle. Black had a fairly straightforward, direct means of attack here (see next note).

24...♞g4

24...♝h3! 25.♞e1 ♜g5 26.♛d4 ♜d8 27.♛h4 ♝f5 28.bxc6 bxc6 29.♛h2 ♜dg8. The concentration of black pieces on the king's wing is such that a human cannot withstand it; the computer itself evaluates the position at 0.00.

25.♛e4 ♛c7 26.g3

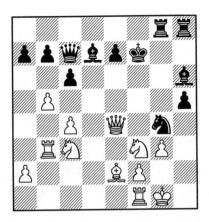

At this point it was hard to find my next move, and I failed to find it. Obviously, it was right here that I should have looked for the solution to the position. All my pieces have taken up their attacking positions, firing full blast at the white king. The blow must be found...

26...♖g6

...and here it is: 26...♗e3‼ 27.fxe3 (27.♔g2 h4 28.♘xh4 ♗xf2 29.♖xf2+ ♘xf2 30.♔xf2 ♕xg3+ 31.♔f1 ♕g1#:

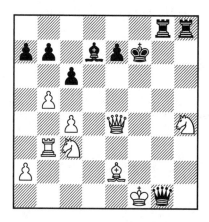

Or 27.♘e5+ ♕xe5 28.♕xe5 ♘xe5 29.fxe3+ ♔e8 30.♔f2 ♘g4+ 31.♗xg4 ♖xg4∓) 27...♕xg3+ 28.♔h1 ♘f6 29.♘e5+ ♔e8 30.♘g4 hxg4+ 31.♕h7 ♖xh7#:

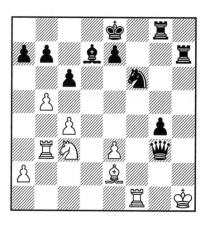

27.♗d3 ♖f6 28.♖e1 ♗f5

White is lost; *Houdini* agrees. Unfortunately, I proved unable to handle the resulting complications.

29.♕e2 ♗xd3?

Now the bishop strike on e3 would only gain strength: 29...♗e3! (threatening ...♕g3) 30.fxe3 ♗xd3 31.♕g2 (31.♕xd3 ♕xg3+ 32.♔h1 ♘f2#) 31...♔g7! (it's strange that Black must shift the focus of the attack from the g- to the f-file) 32.♖b4 ♖hf8−+.

30.♕xd3 h4 31.♘e4 ♘xf2?

31...hxg3!? 32.fxg3 (32.♘xf6 gxf2+) 32...♖g6 33.bxc6 bxc6 34.♕b1 ♘e3 35.♖bxe3 ♗xe3+ 36.♖xe3 ♖h5, and the position remains as sharp as ever.

32.♔xf2 hxg3+ 33.♘xg3

33...♗f4

33...♗d2!?. It's almost impossible to conceive of a mere human finding a move like this. All three results are now possible. This devastating move was suggested by *Houdini*, e.g. 34.♖g1 (forced: 34.♕xd2 ♖h2+ 35.♔f1 ♖xd2−+; 34.♖h1 ♖h1 35.♘xh1 ♕h2+ 36.♔f1 ♕xh1+ 37.♔e2 ♗f4 38.♔f2 ♗d6 39.bxc6 ♗c5+ 40.♔e2 ♕g2+ 41.♔d1 ♖d6−+) 34...♖h2+ 35.♖g2 ♗e1+ 36.♔xe1 ♖xg2.

White has the upper hand here; however, could a human have found all of those moves?

34.♘e4 ♖fh6 35.♔e2 cxb5 36.cxb5 ♖d8 37.♘d4

The final critical moment of the game. Here Black had an easy draw by perpetual check.

37...♕b6?

37...♖h2+ 38.♔f1 (38.♘f2? ♕e5+ 39.♔f1 ♕xd4 40.♕xd4 ♖xd4∓) 38...♖h1+ 39.♔f2 ♖h2+ 40.♔f1 ♖h1+.

38.♖d1 e5 39.♕c4+ ♔g7 40.♘f5+ ♔g6 41.♘xh6 ♕e3+ 42.♖xe3 ♗xe3 43.♖xd8

A tremendous game! White survived. But surely not everyone would have waded safely through so much debris. In such positions, in any case, the winner will be the one with the greater understanding of what's going on. You cannot have victories without defeats!

1-0

56. Grabuzova – Elshad

1.d4 d6 2.c4 ♘d7 3.♘c3 h6 4.e4 c6 5.♗e3

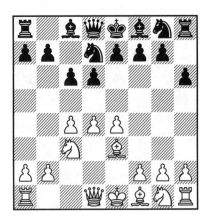

5...♕a5!?

A subtle opening treatment – Black waits until White brings out the knight to f3, then ...g7-g5 will be in the air.

6.♖b1 ♕c7

I might have waited for b2-b4 – for wasn't this exactly why White played her last move, ♖b1 – and only then would I have retreated to c7. I think that including the move b2-b4 favors Black, since Black could then attack this pawn with ...a7-a5. In addition, the a1-h8 diagonal is weakened, and our f8-bishop will soon be occupying it.

7.♘f3 g5 8.♗e2 ♗g7

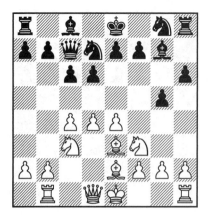

9.0-0

One can understand this vastly experienced chessplayer on a human level: she doesn't want her king to stay in the center for too long. But now Black gets the standard attack for this opening.

9...♘gf6!

The strongest! Black threatens to jump his knight to g4 – what to do? You don't want to play h2-h3, as then the h3-pawn will become the hook that Black's attack will latch onto.

10.♘e1 ♘f8 11.b4 ♘g6 12.g3?

This desire to prevent the knight from landing on f4 or h4 turns out to be a mistake. The weakening of the light squares around the king is considerably worse than the possible knight invasion into the aforementioned squares. Now, what does chess science say? It says that we should not move the pawns in front of our king – especially when our opponent is attacking there. And that we should not advance the pawns where we are weaker. But White is caught in the illusion that she will soon play f2-f4, with an "attack" on Black's king.

12...♗h3 13.♘g2 g4!?

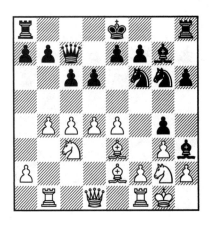

14.f4?

We have already seen, more than once, what this leap into the abyss leads to...

14...gxf3! 15.♗xf3 h5 16.♖e1 h4

16...h4!? 17.♘xh4 ♘xh4 18.gxh4 ♖xh4 19.♗f2 ♖h6 20.♗g3 ♖g6∓.

16...♘g4!? 17.♗c1 h4 18.♗xg4 ♗xg4 19.♕xg4 ♗xd4+ 20.♗e3 ♗xc3 21.♘xh4 ♘e5 22.♕e2 ♗xe1 23.♖xe1 a5∓.

This variation (and the next footnote) show the proper way to play an attack against the white king. Important sketches.

17.♘xh4 ♘xh4 18.gxh4 ♖xh4 19.♗g5

19.♗f2 ♖h6 20.♗g3 ♖g6∓.

19...♖h8 20.b5 ♔f8 21.bxc6 bxc6 22.♗f4 ♘d7

Controlling the dark squares e5 and d4, while targeting the d4-pawn.

23.c5 ♛a5

Compare the opposing kings from a safety standpoint!

24.♘a4 dxc5 25.e5 ♖d8 26.♗xc6 cxd4 27.♖b5 ♛c7 28.♗xd7 ♛xd7 29.♖b4

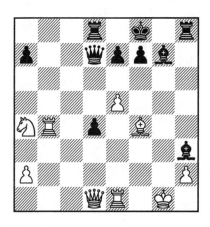

29...♚g8

Here 29...♗h6! is also strong: 30.♗xh6+ ♖xh6 31.♚f2 ♖g6 32.♖xd4 ♛xd4+ 33.♛xd4 ♖xd4 34.♘c5 ♖d5. Black simply has an extra rook, his attack raging undiminished.

30.♘c5 ♛d5 31.♘e4 ♛xa2 32.♖e2 ♛d5 33.♛e1 d3 34.♖d2 ♗f5 35.♛e3 a5 36.♖a4 ♗xe5 37.♛g3+ ♗g7 38.♚f2 ♚f8

38...♗xe4−+.

39.♗c7 ♖a8 40.♖xa5 ♖xa5 41.♗xa5 ♗e5 0-1

Chapter 3

57. Mikhailov – Elshad

Moscow 1999

1.d4 c6 2.c4 ♕a5+ 3.♘c3 g5 4.♘f3

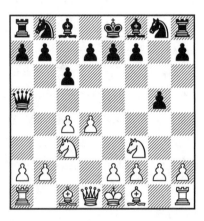

A sharp and unusual position! Besides what happened in the game, here Black has a number of interesting ideas.

4...h6

4...g4!?. A very attractive and strong move! Black immediately asks White to tell where his king's knight is headed: 5.♘d2 ♗g7 6.♘b3 ♕h5. A most original position. How do you play this? No one knows. If White castles short, Black is right there waiting for him! And if long – well, it's hard to prepare for that; and besides, it does look risky. And Black already has a definite plan for bringing out his forces: ...d7-d6, ...♘d7-f8-e6, ...♕h5-g6, and ...h5-h4.

4...♘f6!?. Even this is possible. It has yet to be tested in practice. One possibility: 5.♗xg5 ♘e4 6.♗d2 ♘xd2 7.♕xd2 d6 8.e4 ♗d7 9.♗e2 ♖g8 10.0-0 ♕h5, and Black's attacking chances on the kingside should not be underestimated.

5.e4 d6 6.d5?!

228

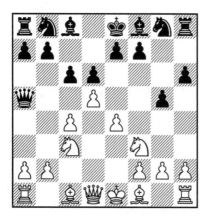

A typical positional error by White, opening up the long diagonal for the black bishop.

6...♘d7 7.♗e3 c5

Now we already know that, as soon as White's dark-squared bishop arrives on e3, we have to play ...♘f6 at once! This is sort of like developing with tempo, because right away we have the threat of ...♘f6-g4, hitting this bishop. White cannot ignore this circumstance: he must play h2-h3 – which, however, gives Black an important hook for his attack with ...g5-g4.

8.♗d3 ♗g7 9.♗d2 ♘f8?!

This standard knight maneuver gives White the chance to get in the e4-e5 break. 9...g4! is far stronger:

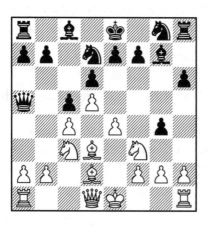

10.♞h4 ♞e5 11.♗e2 ♞f6 12.0-0 h5.

10.0-0

10.e5! dxe5 11.0-0 ♞d7 12.♛e2 ♛c7 13.♖fe1, with initiative for White.

10...♗g4

10...♞g6, with the threat of ...g5-g4, is interesting too: 11.h3 ♗d7 12.a3 ♛c7 13.b4 ♞e5 14.♞xe5 ♗xe5 15.bxc5 ♛xc5 16.♖b1 b6, with complex positional play on the dark squares.

11.♗e2 ♞g6 12.♖e1 ♛c7 13.h3

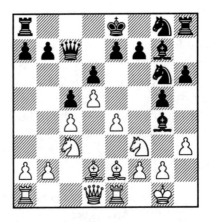

Once again, Black has a wide choice. Among other things, he can retreat the bishop to d7 in order to deliver the nasty blow ...g5-g4.

13...♗xf3

13...♗d7!? 14.♞h2 ♞f6 15.a3 ♞e5 16.b4?! cxb4 17.axb4 ♞xc4 18.♗xc4 ♛xc4 19.♖c1 0-0!∓; 13...♗xc3!? 14.♗xc3 ♗xf3 15.♗xf3 (15. ♗xh8 ♗xe2 16.♛xe2 ♞xh8∓) 15...♞f6 16.♛a4+ ♚f8, and in this complicated position Black's chances are not at all inferior, since in a closed position, Black's two knights are in no way less effective than White's bishops.

14.♗xf3 ♗e5

14...♘e5!?.

15.♕e2 ♘f6 16.a3 ♕d7 17.b4

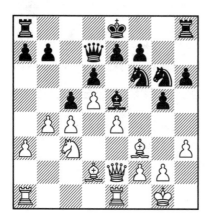

17...h5!?

This leads to a direct attack on the king. There is also a positional alternative – one might say a prophylactic move against White's activity – with ...♖a8-c8, keeping the important point c5 under control and indirectly attacking the c4 square: 17...♖c8 18.bxc5 ♖xc5 19.♖ab1 0-0 20.♖b4 b6 21.♕d3 ♖fc8, and Black keeps a tight grip on the initiative.

18.♖ab1??

The threat of ...g5-g4 is so obvious that it's strange that White ignores it.

18.♕d3 (forced) 18...g4 19.hxg4 hxg4 20.♗d1 ♔f8! (20...♔f8; 20... g3?? 21.♗a4) 21.♖a2 g3 22.f3 ♗d4+ 23.♗e3 ♘f4 24.♕d2 ♖h2 25.♗xd4 ♖xg2+ 26.♕xg2 ♘xg2 27.♔xg2 cxd4 28.♘b5 d3–+ (28...♔g7).

18...g4 19.bxc5 dxc5 20.♖b5 ♘h4! 21.♕d3 gxf3 22.♖xc5 ♖g8

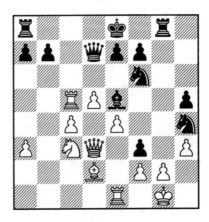

White resigned. A typical picture in the Elshad System. Black's king stands right in its starting spot on e8. Meanwhile, White has "done what he should" – get mated!

0-1

58. S. Shestakov – Elshad

Moscow 1999

1.d4 c6 2.c4 ♕a5+

3.♘c3

3.♗d2 ♕b6 4.♗c3 d5!.

3...d6 4.♘f3 h6 5.e4

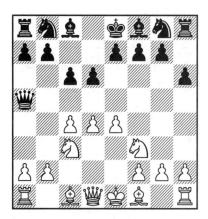

Of course, knowing the sort of troubles that await White now, we could suggest e2-e3 here, shoring up d4. But, since the threat is not apparent to the naked eye, why not take control of the entire center with pawns?!

5...♘d7 6.♗e2 g5 7.h3 ♗g7 8.0-0 ♘f8 9.♗e3 ♘g6

Here 9...♘f6!? is more accurate:

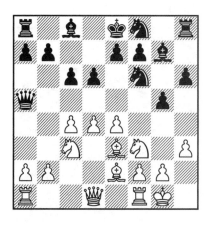

10.d5 g4 11.hxg4 ♘xg4 12.♗d4 ♗xd4 13.♕xd4 ♖g8 14.♖ab1 c5 15.♕d2 ♘g6, and Black's pieces hover threateningly over White's castled position.

10.a3 g4 11.hxg4 ♗xg4 12.b4

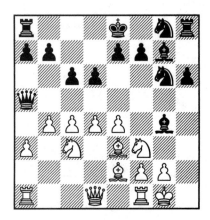

Only "creative searching" could explain this move, for Black's precise purpose when bringing the queen out to a5 is to slide it over to h5!

12...♕c7

12...♕h5!:

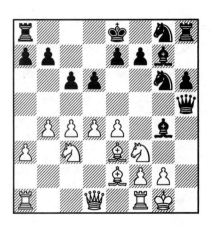

13.♘h2 ♗xe2 14.♕xe2 ♕xe2 15.♘xe2 ♘f6 16.f3 h5 17.♖ab1 h4, and Black's attack on the king persists even with the queens off the board.

13.♖c1 ♘f6 14.b5

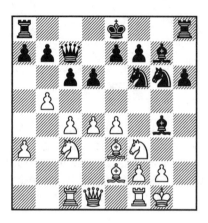

14...♖g8!

The rook goes into ambush, keeping an eye on the white king. There are also the alternatives 14...h5 and 14...♗d7:

1) 14...h5 15.♖b1 h4 16.c5 h3 17.cxd6 ♕d7! 18.bxc6 bxc6 19.♕a4? hxg2 20.♔xg2 ♗xf3+ 21.♗xf3 ♕h3+ 22.♔g1 ♕h2#;

2) 14...♗d7 (with the idea of ...♘f6-g4!) 15.♕c2 ♘g4 16.♗d2 h5 17.♖fe1 h4 18.♗f1 ♕c8, with plenty of play on the kingside.

15.♘h2 ♗d7

15...♗xe2!? 16.♕xe2 h5 17.f4 ♗h6 18.f5 ♗xe3+ 19.♕xe3 ♘f8 20.e5 dxe5 21.dxe5 ♘g4 22.♘xg4 ♖xg4 23.bxc6 bxc6!. It's impossible to pick a winner here.

16.f4 e5!?

A strike on the most fortified of places. Although the engines consider this move weaker than the alternatives, let me offer my own opinion anyway: Elshad is a pioneer. Nobody makes progress without making mistakes, least of all innovators. The idea of this move is to open up the dark squares in the center.

17.dxe5 dxe5 18.bxc6 bxc6 19.f5 ♘f4 20.♗f3 ♗f8!

The bishop redeploys in advance to the a7-g1 diagonal, in case White takes the f4-knight with his bishop. And White can't tolerate that knight at all.

21.♗xf4 exf4 22.e5 ♕xe5! 23.♖e1 ♗c5+ 24.♔h1 ♗e3

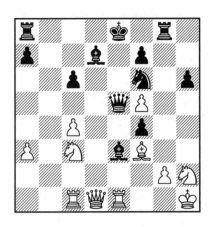

Now we can see just how poorly the white king is protected and how comfortable the black king feels in the center.

25.♕c2 ♗xf5 26.♗xc6+ ♔f8 27.♕a4

27.♗xa8 ♗xc2.

27...♘h5!

Already, Black is threatening mate on the move, with ...♘g3.

28.♘f1 ♘g3+

28...♖g4! 29.♘xe3 ♖h4+ 30.♔g1 fxe3 31.♘e2 ♕h2+ 32.♔f1 ♕h1+ 33.♘g1 ♘g3#:

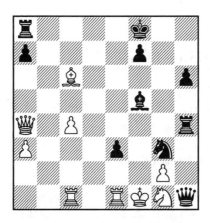

29.♘xg3 ♖xg3 30.♕b4+ ♔g7 31.♘e2 ♖g4 32.♘g1 ♖h4+ 33.♘h3 ♗xh3 34.♖e3 ♕xe3 35.♕b2+ ♔h7 36.gxh3 ♖xh3+ 37.♔g2 ♖g8+

(see diagram next page)

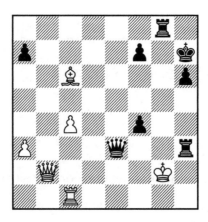

Symbolic – the rook, which has stood *en prise* for so long, is the one who delivers the fatal blow!

38.♔f1 ♖g1# 0-1

59. Andrey Fomin – Elshad

Moscow 2008

This game was played at the Aeroflot Open with a classical time control. Elshad's opponent has an ELO of 2242.

1.d4 d6 2.♘f3 h6 3.c4 g5

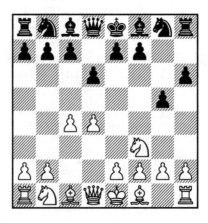

It may be more clever to play ...c7-c6 here – so as not to "scare" White with ...g7-g5 – and give him the chance to occupy the whole center: 3...c6 4.e4 ♘d7 5.♘c3 g5.

4.h3

As a rule, this kind of move is made automatically. The threat of ...g5-g4 looks (and is) dangerous. However, White now must think twice before castling short, since Black will then always have the ...g5-g4 break, wrecking the kingside.

4...♗g7 5.♘c3 ♘d7 6.e4

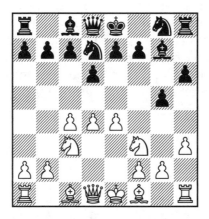

It might have been more solid to play e2-e3; but as a rule, nobody who plays White would be thinking that Black's whole scheme of development is aimed at pressuring the d4-pawn.

6...c6 7.♗e3 ♕a5 8.♗d3 ♘f8

(see diagram next page)

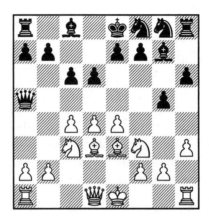

Black develops according to his scheme, which has withstood every test. But for those with inquiring minds – might I suggest a different plan of play – 8...♘gf6 ? The point is that if White castles (and why shouldn't he?), then after ...g5-g4 White is more than likely to capture hxg4, and then we can recapture with the knight and threaten the e3-bishop: 8...♘gf6!? 9.0-0 g4! 10.hxg4 ♘xg4 11.♗f4 ♘f8 12.♗g3 h5 13.♗e2 ♘g6.

9.0-0 g4!

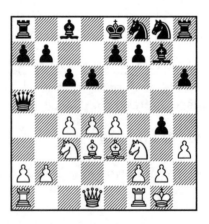

Note that, after this break, the fifth rank is cleared for the queen to swing over to h5. This is one of the most important opening ideas in the Elshad. My tongue just can't bring itself to call this system of play for Black, a "defense"!

10.hxg4 ♗xg4 11.♗e2 ♘g6

Keeping the e3-bishop from going to f4 and then g3 to protect the king. Moreover, it's one more piece to add to the kingside attack.

12.♕b3 ♕c7!

As the base pawn, on which Black's entire pawn chain depends, the b7-pawn is very important.

13.d5 c5!

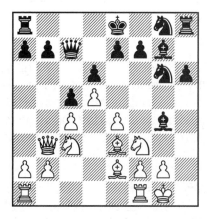

Very well played. The a1-h8 diagonal is in Black's hands, and he nails it down with his last move. If Black doesn't do this now, then White can break with c4-c5, even at the cost of sacrificing a pawn, to disrupt the harmony among Black's pieces.

14.♕a4+

A typical check in the Elshad System. What does White have in mind? Evidently, he expects that this check will prevent Black from castling, or else force him to trade queens. But the black king simply walks over to f8, where it is ideally posted; if need be, it can move up to g7. Meanwhile, White has lost an important tempo. This is a psychological trap into which many fall, even the highest-rated players. Such is the power of cliché – "Stop his king from castling!"

14...♔f8 15.♕c2

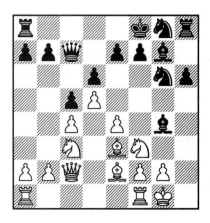

15...♘f6

Well played. Here, though, I want to bring your attention to yet another unconventional treatment of the position: 15...♗xc3. The idea is that, despite trading off our powerful bishop, we gain a few important advantages, clearing the g-file for the attack and bringing the knight out to f6 with tempo (thanks to the threat to the e4-pawn).

Let's see: 15...♗xc3!? 16.♕xc3 ♘f6 17.♕c2 ♕d7 18.♖ab1 ♘xe4! 19.b4 (19.♕xe4 ♗f5) 19...♘g5 20.♘xg5 hxg5 21.bxc5 ♗h3! 22.c6 bxc6 23.dxc6 ♕e6 24.♗f3 ♘e5 25.♗d5 ♗xg2!! 26.♗xe6 ♗f3:

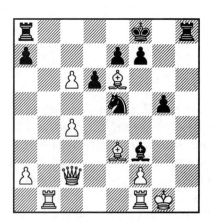

and mate is unavoidable.

16.♘h2 h5!

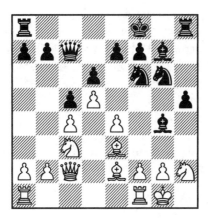

Brilliant! Checkmate is possible not only along the g-file, but on the h-file too, if White takes on g4. And then the black rook that's been standing on h8 will join in the attack without making a move.

17.f3

17.♘xg4 hxg4 18.g3 ♗h6 19.♗xh6+ ♖xh6 20.♔g2 ♔g7 21.♖h1 ♖ah8 22.♖xh6 ♖xh6 23.♖h1 ♖xh1 24.♔xh1 ♕d8 25.♔g2 ♘e5. White's pieces have no moves – and by way of comparison, note how well Black's knight stands on e5!

17...♗d7 18.f4

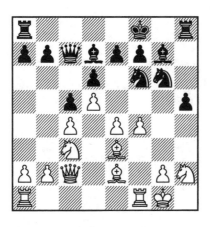

18...♘g4

The push ...h5-h4-h3! is also worth looking into: 18...h4 19.♖ad1 h3 20.g3 ♕c8 21.a3 ♖g8 22.b4 b6! (there's no need to give White any sort of counterplay) 23.bxc5 bxc5 24.♖b1 ♘g4 25.♘xg4 ♗xg4 26.♗xg4 ♕xg4 27.♔h2 ♗xc3 28.♕xc3 ♘e5 29.♗f2 ♘f3+ 30.♔h1 ♘d2, and White cannot hold.

19.♗d2?!

19.♘xg4 suggests itself here, even though opening the h-file looks very dangerous.

19...♗d4+ 20.♔h1 ♘f2+

Picking up the exchange with a continuing attack.

21.♖xf2 ♗xf2 22.♖f1 ♗g3 23.♕d3 ♗xh2

23...h4!? is also very strong: 24.♕f3 ♕b6 25.b3 f6 26.♘g4 ♔f7 27.♘d1 ♖ag8.

24.♔xh2 ♗g4 25.♖f2 ♕d7 26.♗f1 a6 27.b3 ♖e8 28.♘a4 f5 29.♘b6 ♕d8 30.exf5 ♘h4 31.♗c3 ♖h6 32.♘a4 ♘xf5 33.♗e2?

The fatal mistake. But White (as often happens in Elshad's System) was exhausted by this almost incomprehensible battle.

33...e6 34.g3

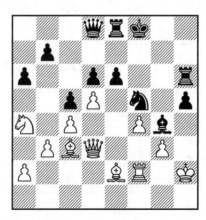

34...h4!

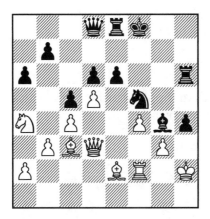

Now White gets mated.

35.♖g2 hxg3+ 36.♔g1 ♕h4 37.♔f1 ♕h1+ 38.♖g1 ♗h3+ 39.♔e1 ♕xg1+ 40.♔d2 g2 41.dxe6 ♖hxe6 0-1

60. Andreyev – Elshad

Moscow 1996

1.c4 c6 2.♘c3 ♕a5 3.d4 g5 4.e4 d6 5.♗e3 ♗g7 6.♗d3?!

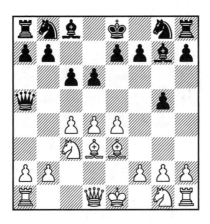

More than once we have said that this bishop, when developed to d3, cuts the natural link between White's queen and the d4-pawn; considering that Black will soon be attacking this pawn, we can see that the bishop has not deployed to its proper position.

6...♘d7 7.♘ge2

This is better than the standard ♘g1-f3, which leaves the knight vulnerable to a pawn attack with ...g5-g4.

7...♘f8 8.0-0 ♘f6!

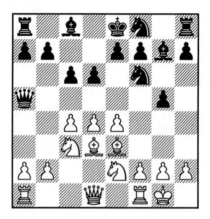

Correct. Now White must somehow protect his bishop against Black's threat of ...♘g4.

9.f3

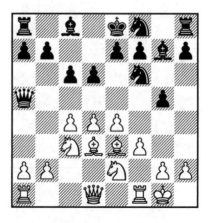

9...♗d7

A bit of a "hiccup." This move is not strictly dictated by necessity. Let's look at Black's other possibilities.

9...♘g6!?:

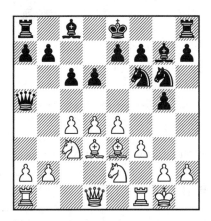

Setting up a pieces-and-pawns assault force on the kingside. Even when he sees the approaching pawn storm with ...h5-h4 and ...g5-g4, White still can't do anything about it. White wishes to strike back in the center (after all, that's what he has been taught), but he can't because the center has shifted. Where to? Let's give that some thought. If Black's pawn were on, say, e5, then the center would stand "where it should," and it could be opened up. Here, though, no matter how badly White might want to, he can't do that.

The breaks with e4-e5 or c4-c5 will be met instantly by capturing on e5 or c5, respectively, while on d4-d5 Black will simply close up the center with ...c6-c5.

Play might continue (9...♘g6) 10.a3 h6 11.b4 ♕c7 12.♕d2 ♘h5 13.c5 dxc5! 14.bxc5 ♘hf4 15.♘xf4 ♘xf4 16.♗xf4 ♕xf4 17.♕f2 ♗e6 18.e5 ♖d8 with a fierce, interesting, complex battle.

9...♘h5!?:

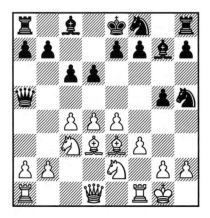

10.♖b1 ♘f4! (exploiting the pawn's loose position on d4) 11.b4 ♕c7 12.♘xf4 gxf4 13.♗f2 ♘g6 14.c5 dxc5 15.bxc5 ♗e6 16.d5 ♗d7!, with an entertaining game where Black enjoys at least even chances.

10.♕d2 h6 11.a3 ♕c7 12.♖ad1 ♖g8 13.♔h1 ♘g6 14.f4

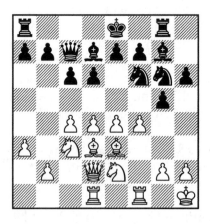

White only seems to have gone over to the attack.

14...e5!?

14...gxf4!? 15.♘xf4 ♘xf4 16.♗xf4 e5 17.dxe5 dxe5 18.♗g3 ♘h5, and Black's attacking chances are superior.

15.dxe5 dxe5 16.fxg5

16.f5?! (trying to lock up the position) 16...♘f4 17.♗g1 0-0-0, and the d-file is vulnerable.

16...hxg5 17.♗xg5

Now what? If 17.g3, stopping the knight from landing on f4, then Black switches to the h-file: 17...♖h8! 18.♔g1 ♘g4 19.♗b1 ♗e6 20.c5 ♘xh2 21.♖f2 ♘g4 22.♖g2 ♗b3 23.♖f1 ♖d8, and it's hopeless for White. Meanwhile, the black king still stands undisturbed on e8!

17...♘g4 18.♘g3 ♖h8 19.h3 f6 20.♘f5 0-0-0 21.♘xg7 fxg5 22.♕xg5?

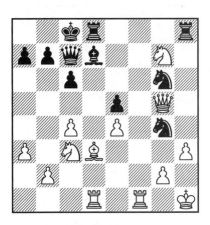

Only here does White stumble for good. We may be able to formulate a general rule: do not open lines for attack against your own king – not even to win material.

22...♘f4 23.♖f3 ♖dg8 24.♔g1

Here it's important to remember that the a7-g1 diagonal is a "death highway." The queen gets to it via b6, and then it's all over.

24...♛b6+ 25.♔f1 ♞h2+ 26.♔e1 ♛g1+ 27.♖f1 ♞xf1 28.♗xf1 ♛e3+ 29.♗e2 ♞d3+

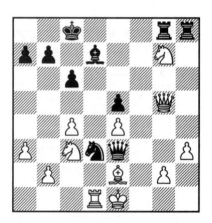

White either gets mated or drops the queen.

0-1

61. *Fritz* 6 – Elshad

2001

This game was against the computer program. Most interesting to see how the program would "refute" the Elshad System.

1.♘f3 d6 2.♘c3

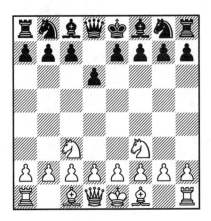

2...♘d7 3.e4 h6 4.d4 g5 5.♗b5?!

Hard to understand the engine here. As Elshad said himself, White probably wanted to "weaken" Black by luring him into playing ...c7-c6, so as to attack the "weakness" on c6 later. One can only smile...

5...♗g7

5...c6!.

6.0-0 c6 7.♗c4 ♘f8 8.♗e3 ♗g4

Provoking the reply h2-h3.

8...♘f6!? is worth a look: 9.h3 g4 10.hxg4 ♘xg4 11.♗d2 ♘e6 12.d5 ♘d4 13.♘xd4 ♗xd4 14.♕e2 ♘e5. Then, at some point, Black's rook goes to g8, with a powerful initiative.

9.h3 ♗e6

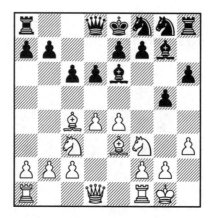

9...♗h5!? 10.♖e1 ♞e6 is also interesting. White could only un-tangle himself with g2-g4, which he would rather not play as it weakens his king considerably.

10.d5 ♗d7!

Under no circumstances will we take on d5 – ever! The c6-pawn must remain on c6 to prevent the white pieces (especially the knight) from reaching d5.

11.♖e1 g4

11...♞g6!? (another good possibility) 12.dxc6 bxc6 13.♗b3 g4 14.hxg4 ♗xg4 15.♕e2 ♞e5 16.♗f4 ♗xf3 17.gxf3 ♕d7.

12.hxg4 ♗xg4 13.dxc6 bxc6 14.♖b1

I really can't explain all of the computer's decisions.

14...♞g6 15.♗e2 ♞f6 16.a3

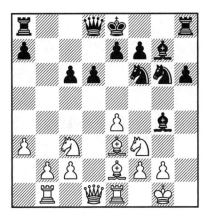

16...♗xf3

16...h5!? (we always keep this idea in mind) 17.♗d4 e5 18.♗e3 ♗h6 19.♗xh6 ♖xh6 20.♕c1 ♘f4 21.g3 ♘xe2+ 22.♘xe2 ♖g6 23.♕e3 ♗xf3 24.♕xf3 ♕b6 25.♖f1 h4 26.♔g2 hxg3 27.♘g3 ♔e7 28.♖h1 ♖ag8∓;

16...♖g8!? 17.b4 ♕c8 18.b5 cxb5 19.♗xb5+ ♔f8 20.♗d4 ♘h5 21.♗xg7+ ♖xg7 22.♘d5 ♘h4 23.♖e3 ♗xf3 24.♖xf3 ♖xg2+ 25.♔f1 ♕g4 26.♕d4 ♖g1+ 27.♔e2 ♕xf3+ 28.♔d2 e5 29.♕d3 ♕xf2+ 30.♔c3 ♖xb1−+.

17.♗xf3 ♔f8 18.b4

Attempting to conquer the d5 square for his knight, after b4-b5.

18...a6 19.a4 h5 20.♗d4 ♘g4 21.♗e2?

21.♗xg7+ merely improves the black king's position: 21...♔xg7 22.b5 axb5 23.axb5 e6! (clearing the way for the queen to shift to the king's wing) 24.bxc6 ♕h4.

21...e5 22.♗e3 ♕h4 23.♕xd6+ ♔g8 24.♗c4 ♘f4 25.♗xf4 ♕xf2+ 26.♔h1 exf4 27.♕xc6

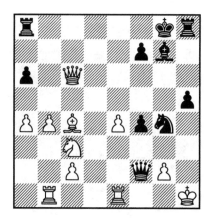

27...♛h4+ 28.♔g1 ♝d4+ 29.♜e3 ♝xe3+ 30.♔f1 ♛f2#

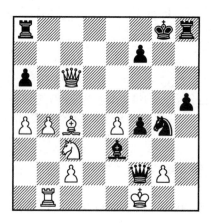

0-1

62. Eannika (2257) – NemtsevIgor (2272)

Live Chess on Chess.com 7/12/2015

1.d4 c6 2.♘c3

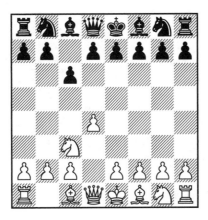

This move order allows Black to enter a Caro-Kann Defense with 2...d5, as there is nothing better than 3.e4 for White. I would consider this transposition to be Black's best option here. But, in order to foster our combative spirit, we must sometimes play the second-best line.

2...d6 3.e4

Of course! Since the c4 square isn't occupied by a pawn, White now has some additional (and good) possibilities compared with the main lines of the Elshad System. For one, he can put his bishop on c4, from where it can eye f7; and for another, in some lines the c2-pawn can go to c3 to protect the d4-pawn.

3...♘d7 4.♘f3 h6 5.♗c4 g5

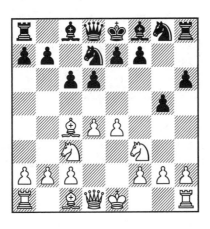

6.h4

A typical reaction by White in this position, in addition to the basic 6.0-0.

6...g4!

The strongest here. Sometimes, in similar situations, ...gxh4 would be a good move, too.

7.♘h2 h5 8.♘f1 ♗g7

8...b5!? (one must always keep this possibility in mind) 9.♗d3 ♗g7 10.♗e3 a6 11.♘g3 c5.

9.♘g3

The knight is headed for f5.

9...♘f8 10.♗g5?!

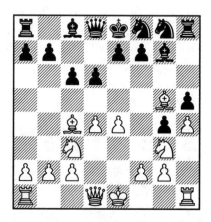

White thinks he is developing his bishop to a safe, solid position. But in fact this is a dubious move, allowing Black to accumulate a couple of important tactical pluses – it weakens the b2-square, while on g5 the bishop will shortly come under attack from the f8-knight, which is following its standard route to e6.

10...♛b6! 11.♘ge2

The right choice. Since he cannot protect both the b- and d-pawns, it's better to shore up the center one.

11...♛xb2!

Simple and strong. When considering whether to grab such pawns (especially the ones they call "poisoned"), the questions to ask are: will the queen get trapped or not; and if not, then will the rook be able to capture on b7 after the queen moves off b2? Here neither of these ideas is possible. The b7-pawn is securely protected by the bishop on c8. Meanwhile, the c3-knight's support has been undermined, which could become a very important factor.

12.♗b3 ♛a3 13.0-0 ♛a5!

Yet another strong and correct move. The queen goes to the fifth rank so as to control all of the squares on it, denying White the chance to play the e4-e5 break. In addition, the g5-bishop is now under attack by Black's queen – a consideration that becomes significant once the f8-knight comes out to e6.

14.♛d2 ♘e6 15.♖ab1

White could also play 15.♗xe6, removing the dangerous knight, which would no longer be around to press against d4 or to hit at the g5-bishop: 15...♗xe6 16.♖ab1 b6 17.♖fd1 ♗c4 18.♘g3 e6, with a complex game where White has no particular compensation for his lost pawn.

15...♘xg5 16.hxg5

16.♛xg5 ♛xg5 17.hxg5 e6!.

16...h4

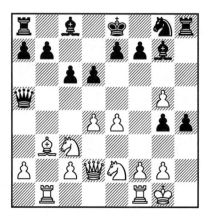

Typically for this system, Black just continues with his attack.

17.♕f4 f6!

Not just defending against the simple threat to take on f7, but also hitting the g5-pawn.

18.♗xg8?! ♖xg8 19.gxf6 ♗xf6

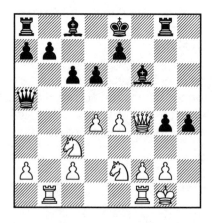

Black has an extra pawn and the bishop pair, and can look forward to an attack on the white king. It's now or never, thinks White, so he launches a desperate assault.

20.e5 dxe5 21.dxe5 ♗xe5

Taking on e5 with the queen is also quite strong, since the endgame would be very depressing for White. But sometimes you simply want to play for mate. This is one of those times.

22.♕c4 ♖h8 23.♖fe1 h3 24.♘d4

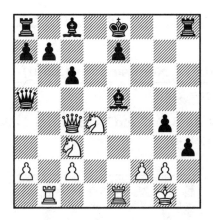

24...g3

It's obvious who is really attacking whose king.

25.fxg3 hxg2 26.♘c6

You cannot even call this a mistake. At any rate, no defense for White can be seen.

26...bxc6 27.♕xc6+ ♔f7 28.♕xa8 ♕c5+

28...♗d4+ wins a bit more quickly: 29.♔xg2 ♗h3+ 30.♔h2 ♗c8+ 31.♔g2 ♖h2+ 32.♔xh2 ♕h5+ 33.♔g2 ♗h3+ 34.♔h2 ♗f1#:

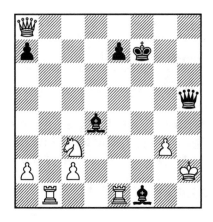

29.♔xg2 ♗h3+ 30.♔h2 ♕f2+ 31.♔h1 ♗g2# 0-1

63. dlp300 (2107) – NemtsevIgor (2200)

Live Chess on Chess.com 6/7/2015

1.d4 c6 2.c4 d6 3.♘c3 ♘d7 4.e4 h6 5.♗e3 g5 6.♕d2 ♗g7 7.♗d3 ♘f8 8.♘ge2 ♘e6

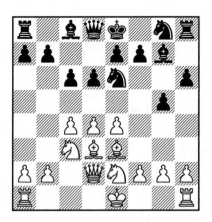

Here, naturally, White starts having doubts. Where to castle? He made the best decision. But later on he defends inaccurately.

9.0-0 ♘f6

Threatening ...♘g4.

10.f3

10.♘g3!? ♘g4 11.♗e2 ♘xe3 12.fxe3, with complicated play (not 12.♕xe3?? ♗xd4).

10...♘h5 11.d5

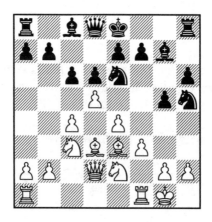

11...♘f8

11...♘ef4!? – this natural-enough move is very good: 12.♘xf4 ♘xf4 13.♗xf4 gxf4 14.♕xf4 ♕b6+ 15.♔h1 ♕xb2 16.♘e2 ♗e5 17.♕h4 ♕b6 18.♖ab1 ♕e3 19.♖bd1 ♖g8∓. Clear advantage to Black thanks to the two bishops; the dark-squared bishop is especially strong.

12.f4

White is caught in a web of illusion. He thinks that he is starting an attack on the black king. Black's next move is his super-weapon in the Elshad System. Remember it!

12...♘g6!

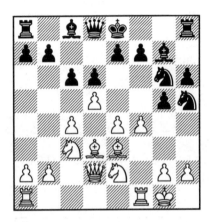

13.fxg5

13.f5 does close up the game and it defends White against mate, for a while. However, all of the dark squares on the long diagonal are now in Black's hands (13...♘e5 14.h3 c5!).

13...hxg5 14.♗xg5 ♘e5 15.♘f4 ♛b6+

This is the key move of the whole system.

16.♛f2

16.♖f2 ♘g4 17.♘xh5 ♖xh5 18.♘d1 ♘xf2 19.♘xf2 ♛xb2−+; or 16.♔h1 ♘g3#:

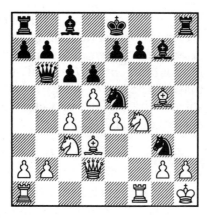

16...♘xf4 17.♗xf4 ♘xd3

Fittingly, White perished precisely because of his d3-bishop!

0-1

64. Skoryak – Amannazarov

1.e4 c6 2.d4 d6 3.♘c3 ♕a5 4.♗d3

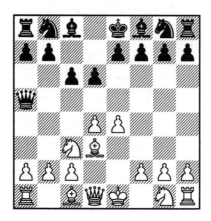

4...g5

Chapter 3

It is an honor – and, at the same time, a difficult proposition – to annotate the games of my publisher (and simultaneously, my friend) Murad Amannazarov. He is a great fan of this opening, and this game was played in a tournament at a classical time control against a good candidate master. The move ...g7-g5, minus the preparatory ...h7-h6, is in the spirit of the system's very creator, Elshad. In fact, one may do entirely without ...h7-h6.

5.♘ge2

We already know that it's much better for White to place this knight on e2 than on f3. Why? Simple: on f3, the knight comes under attack with ...g5-g4, after which it has no good retreat squares, and the d4-pawn is deprived of a defender.

5...♗g7 6.0-0 g4!

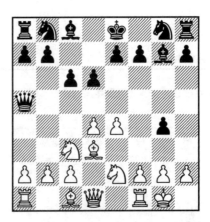

Correct! The logic of Black's treatment is as follows: the pawn has moved forward, enabling the queen to shoot over to h5 to attack the white king. If the white knight goes to g3, then the h-pawn can kick it with ...h7-h5-h4 and continue with ...h4-h3.

7.♗e3

White has developed his pieces harmoniously. What next? What does White play for? What's his strategy? This is White's chief problem in this opening.

7...h5 8.a3 h4 9.b4

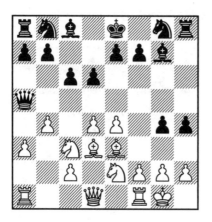

9...♕c7

9...♕h5?! 10.♘f4 ♕h7 11.e5. Unfortunately, in this concrete situation, the queen shuttle to h5 is a no-go; but there is another way...

10.♖b1 ♘d7 11.♗c4 ♘f8 12.b5 ♘f6 13.d5?!

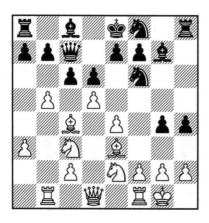

A typical positional mistake by White: giving up the e5 square while getting nothing in return.

13...c5!

The strongest, not allowing White's pieces access to d4.

14.a4 ♘g6 15.♕d2 ♘e5! 16.♗b3 h3!

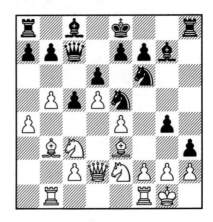

Simple and strong! The threat of ...♘f3+, forking, keeps White from preventing the collapse of his king's abode!

17.f4 hxg2 18.fxe5 gxf1♕+ 19.♖xf1 dxe5 0-1

65. I. Naumkin – I. Nemtsev

Aeroflot Open, Moscow 4/15/2014

1.d4 c6 2.c4 d6 3.♘f3 ♘d7 4.♘c3 h6 5.e4 g5 6.♗e2 ♗g7 7.0-0 ♘f8

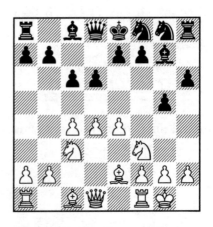

This is a sort of *tabiya* for this system. The knight's maneuver to f8 has the power to confuse anyone, even an experienced grandmaster. He stared fixedly at me, grinned, said, "I've never seen anything like this," and started to think how to punish me for this impudence. Since the knight has gone to f8, well, then it must come out to e6 – the grandmaster was probably thinking. So, let's just stop him going there:

8.d5?!

If only he'd known that I was just feinting at going to e6, in order to induce him to play this!

8...c5

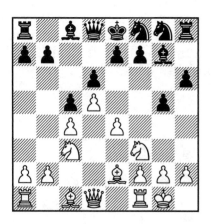

OK, he's helped me to get my knight to e5 via g6, and I thank him for that. 8...c5 isn't the only way to go in this system. Elshad himself leaves the pawn on c6 in order to have the possibility of moving his queen out to b6. But I – not without reason – feared White's c4-c5, which, it seemed to me, would disrupt the harmony of the black pieces as capturing on c5 would destabilize Black's position in the center.

8...♘g6 9.c5 dxc5.

9.♗d2

9.♖b1 ♗xc3 10.bxc3.

9...♘g6

9...♗xc3 10.♗xc3 f6; 9...♕a5.

10.♘e1

I could not believe my eyes. Was it possible that a grandmaster could believe that he was preparing f2-f4?

10...♘f6 11.♘d3 ♘d7 12.f4?!

Beyond a doubt, this is a positional mistake. The engine grants White the advantage everywhere; but that's normal for this system. Everybody wants to punish Black – even the computer! Thing is, the e5 square now comes under Black's complete control. Here, in addition to the text move, Black also had 12...♗d4+ and then not taking on f4, in Elshad's spirit.

12...gxf4

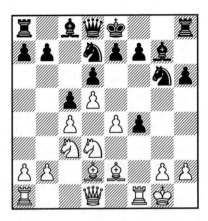

As we said, besides this clean positional continuation, leading to the capture of the e5 square, there is also the possibility of playing for mate with 12...♗d4+:

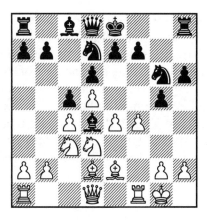

13.♔h1 ♘f6 14.fxg5 hxg5 15.♗xg5 ♘e5 16.♖c1 ♘eg4 17.♗xg4 ♘xg4 18.b4 ♖xh2#. Although this variation was certainly cooperative, it clearly shows Black's attacking methods against the white king in the Elshad.

13.♘xf4

13.♗h5 ♗d4+ 14.♔h1 ♘de5 15.♗xg6 ♘xd3 (15...♘xg6 16.♘xf4 ♘xf4 17.♗xf4 ♗xc3 18.bxc3 f6 19.♖b1 h5 20.♕d2 ♕a5 21.♗h6 ♕c7, and chances are dynamically equal: 21...♕a4 22.♗g7 ♖h7 23.♗f6 exf6 24.♖xf6 ♗g4 25.♖xd6 ♖f7 26.h3; 21...♗g4 22.h3) 16.♗h5 ♘f2+ 17.♖xf2 ♗xf2 18.♗xf4 ♗d4.

13...♘xf4 14.♗xf4 ♕b6

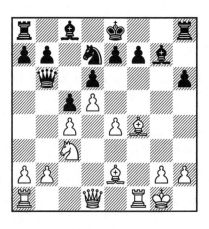

Chapter 3

This is a very important link in Black's plan. The queen goes out to b6, hitting b2, a threat that White cannot ignore. Also, in some variations, the d8 square is cleared for the king; on the other hand, in the present game, Black's doesn't make use of it – which becomes a sort of general discovery. It turns out that the king can stay in the center, confusing his opponent, who won't know where to direct his pieces, how to play. This is the same as if a person falls into a country where they speak a language unlike any language he knows: there's nobody to talk to and he can't find out anything from anyone.

15.♖b1 ♗e5

Here Black has other good choices: 15...♖g8, setting up a direct mating attack along the g-file; or 15...♘e5, taking over a commanding height (16.♗g3 h5).

16.♗h5 ♗xf4

16...♖h7!?.

17.♖xf4

This is the only time in this game where I had to calculate a variation.

17...♖f8

Unfortunately, 17...♘e5 doesn't work: 17...♘e5 18.♗xf7+ ♘xf7 19.♕h5 ♖f8 20.♖xf7 (20.♖bf1) 20...♖xf7 21.♖f1 ♗g4 22.♕xf7+ ♔d7 23.e5+−; nor does 17...♘f6 18.♖xf6 exf6 19.e5 fxe5 20.♘e4.

White is so confused. If we take a look at his pieces now, it's easy to see that they are completely unable to cooperate with one another – it's every man for himself. Soon, the weakening of the dark-square periphery near the white king will become important. The opening of the position is a direct mistake by White. Let's think a little: if opening up the game favors the better-developed side, is that what White has here? He only has a few scattered pieces out in play; meanwhile, the a7-g1 diagonal is wide open.

18.♘a4 ♛a6

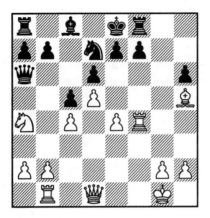

19.b4?! cxb4 20.♖xb4 ♛a5

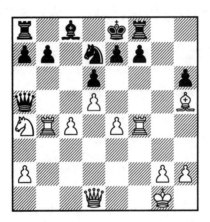

Black's dark-square strategy in action! Doubtlessly, the grandmaster was "attacking" me at the moment; but it would have been very difficult for him to see how he was leaving his own king weak.

21.♖b5 ♛c7 22.♛d4

Pretty much forced, as the c4-pawn was under attack. Now White's advantage looks absolute! But in fact it's nothing more than an optical illusion. By now, even *Houdini* grants Black the upper hand. Finally! The white pieces remind me of a soap bubble sitting on the surface, ready to pop.

22...♞e5!

That gorgeous knight has taken its place. Sometimes, in this opening, the knight alone is worth more than all the white pieces put together.

23.c5 ♝d7

The black trampoline begins to spring back up!

24.♜b1 ♜g8!

Already eyeing the g2 square.

25.♜f2 ♝g4 26.♝xg4 ♞xg4

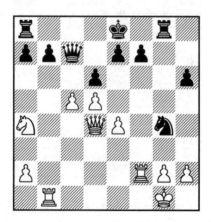

27.♜f4

The only move, in view of the threat ...dxc5, when Black's queen takes on h2!

27...f6!

Very strong! This creates both a possible spot for the king on f7 and, more importantly, a support for the e5-pawn.

28.cxd6 ♕xd6 29.♕d2

Again forced, this time due to the threat of ...e6-e5.

29...♖c8 30.h3 ♘e5

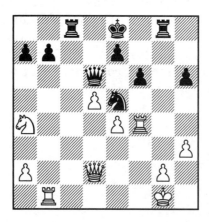

By this point, the GM was already in serious time pressure; this comes as no surprise, since the master had broken all of the "rules" of chess and left White no place to move. What followed was a kamikaze assault.

31, ♖xb7?? ♕a3 32.d6

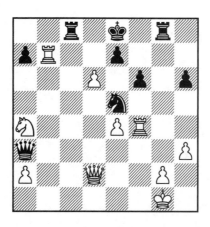

Chapter 3

32...♖c1+ 33.♕xc1

He must give up his queen, as 33.♔h2 ♕g3 is mate.

**33...♕xc1+ 34.♖f1 ♘f3+ 35.♔f2 ♕d2+ 36.♔xf3 ♕xg2+
0-1**

GM Naumkin resigned. We spent another 20 minutes on the post-mortem, and it looked to me as though everything was pretty convincing. But my opponent's feelings of disappointment apparently hadn't left him; according to what our mutual friends told me afterwards, he was saying later that "this Nemtsev was making use of some sort of help, probably computer" – it couldn't be that you could play like that and beat a grandmaster.

Chapter 4

//

Shadow of the Dragon:
White Castles Queenside

66. humorous (2589) – Nemtsev_Igor (2599)

1/11/2015

　　1.d4 c6 2.c4 d6 3.♘c3 ♘d7 4.♘f3 h6 5.e4 g5 6.♗e3 ♗g7
7.h4 g4! 8.♘d2 ♘f8 9.♗e2 h5 10.f3 ♘f6

　　10...gxf3 11.gxf3 ♕b6 12.♘b3 ♗h6 13.♗xh6 ♘xh6 14.♕d2 a5
15.0-0-0 a4 16.♘a1 a3 17.b3 f5 18.♔b1 fxe4 19.fxe4 ♗g4.

　　11.e5 dxe5 12.dxe5 ♘6d7

　　12...gxf3!? 13.gxf3 ♘g8 14.f4 ♘h6 15.♘f3 ♘g4! 16.♕xd8+ ♔xd8
17.♖d1+ ♔c7 18.♗d2 f6 19.exf6 ♗xf6.

　　13.f4 ♘e6 14.g3 ♘dc5 15.♕c2 ♘d4 16.♗xd4 ♕xd4 17.0-0-0
♕e3 18.♖hg1 ♗e6 19.♔b1 b5 20.cxb5 cxb5 21.♗xb5+ ♔f8
22.♘f1 ♕xg1 23.f5 ♗xe5

　　23...♗d7-+ 24.♗xd7 ♘xd7.

　　24.fxe6 ♘xe6 25.♕e4 ♗xc3 26.♕xa8+ ♔g7 27.♕b7 ♗f6
28.♗c4 ♘d4 29.♕d5 e6 30.♕d7 ♖d8 31.♕xa7 ♕f2 32.♕b7
♕c2+ 0-1

67. Chuchkalov_Sergei – Nemtsev_Igor

2/22/2015

　　1.d4 c6 2.c4 d6 3.♘c3 ♘d7 4.e4 h6 5.♘f3 g5 6.♗e2 ♗g7

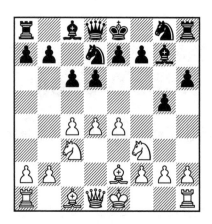

7.h4

One more attempt at a refutation. It's a move that, though it looks strong, is actually weak. Here it's very important to understand the situation of the d4-pawn: it is the weakest pawn in White's pawn center, as neither the c- nor the e-pawn can defend it any longer, because they themselves have already advanced to the fourth rank. In order to stay on d4, it needs to be supported by pieces. Thus it depends on the queen and the f3-knight. Therefore, all Black needs to do is to play ...g5-g4 to drive away that defender. Incidentally, the knight has no good retreat squares.

7...g4 8.♞g1

8.♞d2 is even worse. Giving up the d4-pawn for the g4-pawn is not an even trade: 8.♞d2 ♗xd4 9.♗xg4 ♞gf6 10.♗f3 (10.♗e2 ♖g8 11.0-0 ♞e5) 10...♞e5 11.♞b3 ♗xc3+ 12.bxc3 a5!?.

8...h5

Somewhat clichéd. 8...♛b6 or 8...c5! are much more in the spirit of the position:

8...♛b6 9.♗e3 ♛xb2.

8...c5!? 9.d5 (9.dxc5 ♞xc5 10.♗xg4 ♗xc3+ 11.bxc3 ♞xe4 12.♛d4 ♞gf6 13.♗xc8 ♖xc8) 9...♗xc3+ 10.bxc3 ♛a5 11.♛c2 ♞gf6 12.♖b1 a6 13.♗d2 ♖b8 14.f4 b5 with counterplay.

9.♗g5

White has obvious problems developing, but this bishop sortie is nearly always bad. The problem is that it takes away the b2-pawn's defender.

9...♛b6

A double attack: the d4-pawn is besieged in every line of this opening. This pawn is the target of Black's opening setup.

10.♞a4

10.♗e3 c5 11.dxc5 ♛xb2–+.

10...♛xd4 11.♛xd4 ♗xd4 12.f3 ♞f8

12...♞e5! 13.0-0-0 c5 14.♞c3 ♗xc3 15.bxc3 f6 16.♗f4 ♞h6 17.♗xh6 ♜xh6 18.f4 ♞c6.

13.0-0-0 ♞e6 14.fxg4?

A tactical oversight. But White is already down a pawn and his position is worse, in any case. An unusual setup. To come to grips with it, in all of its myriad subtle interconnections, would not be realistic in a practical game.

14...hxg4 15.♗xg4 ♞xg5 16.♗xc8 ♗e3+ 17.♔c2 ♜xc8 18.♞e2 ♞e6 19.g4 b5 20.♞ac3

20.cxb5 cxb5+ 21.♞ac3 b4.

20...bxc4 21.♜h3 ♗c5 22.♜f1 ♞f6 23.g5 ♞xg5 0-1

68. megaman666 (2763) – MASTER-GURU(2788)

4/23/2014

1.♞f3 d6 2.c4 c6 3.♞c3 ♞d7 4.d4 h6 5.e4 g5 6.h3 ♗g7 7.♗e3 ♞f8 8.♛d2

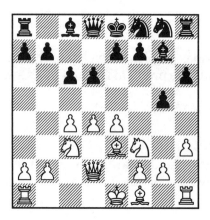

A fairly popular deployment against Elshad's System. White castles long, and the setup starts to resemble two other systems:

1) the Sämisch Attack in the King's Indian Defense; and

2) the Dragon Sicilian.

The key difference is that Black will not be castling kingside. This means that only Black will be attacking, since White has no targets for his own attack.

8...♘e6 9.0-0-0 ♕a5 10.♔b1 ♘f6

Black also has another choice that may be even stronger: 10...c5!:

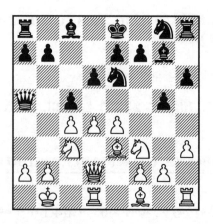

11.d5 (11.♗e2 ♖b8 12.♖he1 ♗d7 13.dxc5 ♗xc3 14.♕xc3 ♕xc3 15.bxc3 ♗a4 16.♖d2 ♘f6 17.cxd6 ♘xe4 18.♖d3 ♘xd6⇄) 11...♗xc3! (11...♘f8 12.e5 ♘g6 13.exd6 ♗xc3 14.♕xc3 ♗f5+ 15.♔a1 ♕xc3 16.bxc3 exd6⇄) 12.bxc3 ♘f8 13.♗d3 ♘d7 14.♔a1 ♘gf6 15.♕c2 a6 16.♖b1 ♖b8⇄. As the preceding variations show, Black always gets excellent play.

11.g3 a6 12.♗g2 b5 13.d5?!

White didn't guess right. 13.e5! had to be played, with a full-blooded game.

13...b4! 14.dxe6 bxc3 15.exf7+ ♔xf7 16.♕c2

16.♕xc3 ♕xc3 17.bxc3 ♘xe4. Even after the queens are traded, the white king is still under attack.

16...♘xe4 17.♕xe4??

Of course this is a terrible blunder, but I never get tired of repeating this: the problems Black sets his opponent in this opening are so difficult that there comes a point when White simply fails to realize what is happening on the board.

17...♗f5–+ 18.♘e1 ♗xe4+ 19.♗xe4 cxb2 20.♗d4 ♗xd4 21.♖xd4 ♕c3 22.♘c2 ♖ab8 23.♖hd1 ♖hf8 24.♗xc6 ♔g7

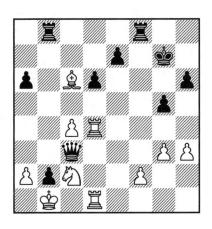

A paean to his dark-square strategy! All of Black's pieces are standing on dark squares.

25.♖1d2 a5 26.f3 ♖xf3 27.♗xf3 ♕xf3 28.♖4d3 ♕f1+ 29.♖d1 ♕xh3 30.♖b3 ♖xb3 31.axb3 ♕xg3 32.♔xb2 h5 33.♖d5 h4 34.♘d4 ♔f6 35.♖f5+ ♔g6 36.♖xa5 h3 37.♘f5 ♕f2+ 38.♔a3 ♕xf5 0-1

69. Algernon (2329) – MASTER_GURU (2349)

11/6/2013

1.d4 d6 2.e4 c6 3.♗d3 ♘d7 4.c3 h6 5.f4

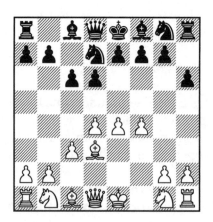

Or 5.♘e2 g5 6.♘g3 ♗g7 (6...♕c7 7.0-0 e5 8.b3 ♘e7 9.♘h5 *[9.♗a3 ♘g6 10.♘d2 ♘f6 11.♘c4 ♗e6 12.♘f5 ♖d8 13.♘fxd6+ ♗xd6 14.♗xd6 ♖xd6 15.dxe5 ♖xd3 16.♕xd3 ♗xc4 17.♕xc4]* 9...♘g6 10.♗a3 ♗e7 11.♘g7+ ♔f8 12.♘f5 ♘f6 13.♘d2 ♗e6 14.♘xe7 ♘xe7 15.♗c4 ♔g7) 7.♘f5.*

5...g5 6.fxg5 ♗g7 7.gxh6 ♘xh6 8.♘f3 ♘f8 9.♕e2 ♘e6 10.♗e3 ♘g4 11.♘bd2 ♘xe3 12.♕xe3 ♗h6 13.♕e2∓ b5

13...c5!? 14.dxc5 ♘f4 15.♕f1 ♖g8 16.g3 ♗h3 17.♗b5+ ♔f8 18.♕f2 ♘g2+ 19.♔d1 a6 20.♗a4 dxc5∓; 13...♘f4 14.♕f1 c5 15.g3 ♗h3 16.♗b5+ (16.♕f2 ♘xd3+) 16...♔f8 17.♕f2 ♘g2+.

14.0-0-0 ♕a5

14...b4! 15.c4 ♕b6 16.♕f2 c5 17.d5 ♘f4 18.♗c2 ♖g8 19.g3 b3 20.axb3 (20.♘xb3 ♘d3+) 20...♘d3+ 21.♗xd3 ♕xb3 22.♗c2 ♕a2 23.♗b1 ♕xc4+ 24.♗c2 ♖b8.

15.♔b1 ♗d7 16.♘b3 ♕b6 17.d5 ♘c5

17...♘f4! 18.♕c2 c5 19.♘c1 ♖b8 20.h4 c4 21.♗f1 ♘h5 22.♘e2 b4.

18.♘xc5 ♕xc5 19.dxc6 ♗xc6 20.e5 0-0-0 21.exd6 ♖xd6 22.♗e4 ♖e6 23.♖d4 ♗g7?

23...f5–+ 24.b4 ♖xe4 25.♖xe4 ♗xe4+ 26.♕xe4 fxe4 27.bxc5 exf3 28.gxf3 ♗e3.

24.♖hd1 ♗xd4 25.♖xd4 ♖h5

25...♗xe4+ 26.♖xe4 ♕f5 27.♘d2 ♖xe4 28.♕xe4 ♕xe4+ 29.♘xe4 ♖xh2–+.

26.♕c2 ♗xe4 27.♖xe4 ♖xe4 28.♕xe4 ♕f5 29.♕xf5+ ♖xf5 30.♔c2 e5 31.♔d3 f6 32.♔e4 ♖f4+ 33.♔e3 ♔d7 34.h4 ♔e6 35.b3 ♖g4 36.c4 bxc4 37.bxc4 ♖xc4 38.♔d3 ♖g4 0-1

70. Vovan1966 (2281) – Nemtsev_Igor (2833)

2/27/2015

1.d4 c6 2.c4 d6 3.♘c3 ♘d7 4.e4 h6 5.♘f3 g5 6.♗e2 ♗g7 7.♗e3 ♘f8 8.♕c2 ♘g6 9.h3 ♘f6 10.0-0-0

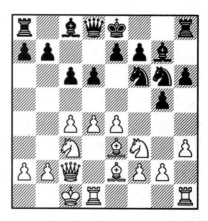

A position often seen in the Elshad. If Black castles short here, then we have a real race along the lines of the Sicilian Dragon. But Black refrains from castling, instead launching at once into the attack.

It's not easy to break up the white king's position. We need to do some maneuvering first.

10...♛a5

The most natural move. Surprisingly enough, there's also 10... g4!?:

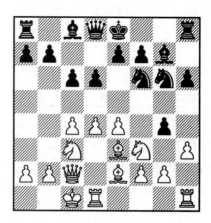

11.hxg4 ♘xg4 12.♔b1 ♘xe3 13.fxe3, with complex play and good prospects for Black.

11.♔b1 ♘h5?!

A loss of time. Objectively speaking, this isn't the best move, either. After the simple 12.g3, Black will have to retreat. Absent 12.g3, then the black knight could land on f4.

12.g3 ♘f6 13.♘d2 ♘f8 14.♘b3 ♕c7 15.f4

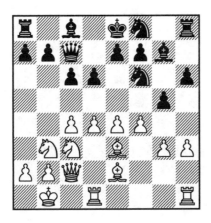

White's position looks (and in fact is) very strong. But he still has to bring the point home. Now Black misses a good chance for counterplay with ...a7-a5-a4.

15...♘e6

15...a5!? 16.♘c1 a4 17.e5 ♘6d7 18.♘a4 c5, and the whole struggle lies ahead – although we must admit that White still has the advantage.

16.d5 ♘f8

Remember: in such positions, we never take on d5, but leave the pawn on c6 so that it controls both d5 and b5 against invasion by the opposing pieces, particularly the knight.

17.fxg5 hxg5 18.♗xg5

Nobody has outlawed greed yet. White loses the lion's share of his advantage. The e5 square now becomes the key square!

18...c5

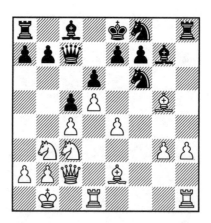

19.♗f4 ♘8d7 20.g4 a6 21.♗d3 b5 22.cxb5? ♕b6

22...c4 23.♘d4 (23.♘e2 axb5) 23...cxd3 24.♕xd3 axb5 25.♘dxb5 ♕a5. Black has not only an extra piece, but also the attack!

23.bxa6 ♗xa6 24.♗xa6 ♕xa6 25.♕e2? c4?

A mistake – although I didn't want to trade queens, this was the right moment to do that as Black already has the upper hand: 25...♕xe2!? 26.♘xe2 ♘xe4 (threatening a fork on f2) 27.♖df1 ♘b6 28.♗c1 ♘xd5.

26.♘d4 ♘c5 27.♘db5 0-0!!

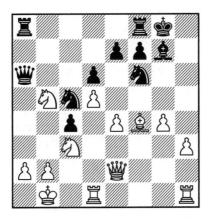

We rarely castle in Elshad's System; but here it's an outstanding move, putting the sleeping rook to work in the attack.

28.♘c7 ♛a5 29.♘xa8 ♜xa8 30.g5?

30.♛xc4 ♜b8 31.e5 (31.♗c1 ♘fd7) 31...♘fd7 32.exd6 (32.e6 ♜xb2+ 33.♔xb2 ♘b6) 32...♜xb2+ 33.♔xb2 ♘b6−+.

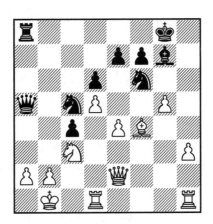

30...♘fxe4−+ 31.♗d2 ♗xc3 32.♗xc3 ♛xa2+ 33.♔c2 ♛b3+ 34.♔c1 ♘xc3

34...♜a1#.

35.♛c2 ♜a1+ 36.♔d2 ♘5e4+ 0-1

71. Fedorov_Alexei (2513) – Nemtsev_Igor (2844)

5/7/2015

1.e4 c6 2.d4 d6 3.c4 h6 4.♘c3 g5 5.♗e3 ♗g7 6.♕d2 ♘d7 7.0-0-0

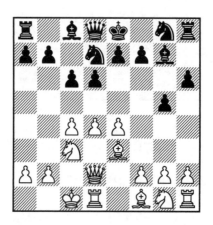

7...♕a5! 8.♔b1 b5

8...a6!? 9.♘f3 b5 10.c5 dxc5 11.dxc5 ♗xc3 12.♕xc3 ♕xc3 13.bxc3 ♘gf6.

9.cxb5 cxb5 10.♘xb5 ♕xd2 11.♖xd2 ♔f8 12.h4 g4

12...♘gf6!? 13.f3 g4.

13.h5 a6 14.♘c7 ♖a7 15.♘d5 e6 16.♘c3 ♘e7 17.♗e2 ♖b7 18.♗xg4 ♘b6 19.♗e2 ♖b8 20.♘f3 ♘c6 21.a3 ♘a5 22.♔a2 ♘ac4 23.♗xc4 ♘xc4 24.♖c2 ♗b7

24...♘xe3!? 25.fxe3 ♖g8, with compensation.

25.b3 ♘a5 26.♖b1 ♔e7 27.b4 ♘c4 28.♖bc1 d5 29.exd5 exd5 30.♖d1 ♖hc8 31.♔b3 ♗c6 32.♘e5 ♘xe5 33.dxe5 ♗xe5 34.♘xd5+ ♔e6 35.♘f4+ ♔f5 36.♖xc6 ♖xc6 37.♘d5 ♔g4 38.♗c5 ♔xh5

38...♖xc5.

39.♘e7 ♖e6

39...♖xc5.

40.♖d5 ♔g4 41.♔c4 ♖b7 42.♘g8 h5 43.♘h6+ ♖xh6 44.♖xe5 h4 45.♖e4+ ♔f5 46.♖d4 ♖c7 47.a4 ♖e6 48.b5 a5 49.b6 ♖xb6 50.♖xh4 ♖b4+ 51.♔d5 ♖xh4 0-1

72. Ilya Khalilov – Vasily Papin

1.e4 c6 2.d4 d6 3.♘f3 h6 4.c4 g5 5.♘c3 ♗g7 6.♗e2 ♘d7 7.♗e3 ♘f8 8.♘d2 ♘g6

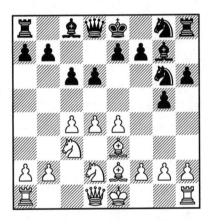

This future grandmaster, being I think just 10 or 11 years old at the time, plays the variation beautifully! Elshad himself said that, after giving Vasily just one or two lessons, he was already playing it very well.

9.g3?!

The light squares are already weakened.

9...e5!?

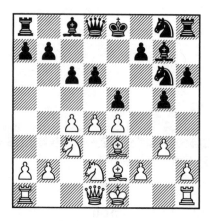

This is another one of the many, many ideas that Elshad introduced in the opening that bears his name.

9...♗h3!? 10.♕c2 ♘f6 11.0-0-0 ♘g4 12.♗xg4 ♗xg4 13.f3 ♗d7 14.♔b1 b5, and Black continues with his offensive – this time on the queenside! The attack's outlines very much resemble the Sämisch variation of the King's Indian.

10.d5 c5 11.♘b5?! ♘8e7 12.h4 gxh4 13.gxh4 ♕b6 14.♕c2 a6 15.♘c3 ♗d7 16.0-0-0 0-0-0 17.h5 ♘f4 18.♘f3 f5 19.♖dg1 ♖hg8 20.♘h4 ♘xe2+ 21.♕xe2 f4 22.♗d2 ♗f6

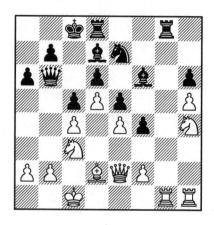

23.♘f3

23.♘g6!? ♘xg6 24.♖xg6 ♖xg6 25.hxg6 ♗g5 would lead, after all is said and done, to the loss of a pawn.

23...♖g4 24.♖xg4 ♗xg4 25.♘a4 ♕c7 26.♔b1 ♔b8 27.♕d3 b5 28.cxb5 c4 29.♕c3 axb5 30.♘h2 ♗e2 31.♕b4 ♗d3+ 32.♔a1 ♗xe4 33.♖c1 ♕b7 34.♘c3 ♗xd5

After 34...♘xd5! 35.♘xd5 ♕xd5, one gets the impression that there are only black pieces on the board!

35.♘xb5 ♘c6 36.♕a4 ♗e6 37.♘c3 d5 38.f3 ♘d4 39.♖d1 ♗f5 40.a3 ♗c2 41.♕b4 ♕xb4 42.axb4 ♗xd1

Of course, the winner of this game could do a better job of commenting on it than I could.

0-1

Chapter 5

//

Miscellaneous Deviations For Both Sides

73. agito (2826) – Nemtsev_Igor (2829)

2/8/2015

1.c4 c6 2.♘c3 ♕a5 3.d4 g5 4.♗d2 h6 5.h4

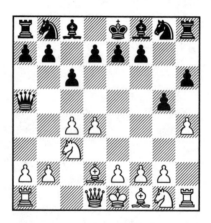

5...gxh4

The scrappiest line. Nonetheless, the more positional 5...g4 is quite playable, as is 5...♗g7.

For example, 5...g4:

(see diagram next page)

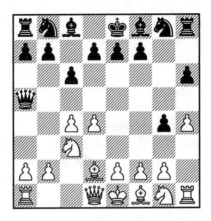

6.e4 d6 7.♗d3 ♗g7 8.♘ge2 ♗d7, with counterplay.

Or 5...♗g7 6.hxg5 hxg5 7.♖xh8 ♗xh8 8.e3 d6 9.♕h5 ♗g7 10.♕h7 ♔f8!, with an extremely confusing game.

6.♖xh4

White might choose to win the pawn back a different way with 6.♘f3 d6 7.♘xh4 ♕b6 8.e3 ♕xb2 9.♖b1 ♕a3 10.♗d3 ♘f6 11.♖b3 ♕a6 12.c5 (12.♕e2 c5!?, with mutual chances after 13.dxc5 ♘bd7! 14.cxd6 ♕xd6 15.♘f5 ♕b8 16.♔f1 ♘c5! 17.♖b1 ♕e5!) 12...♕xd3 13.♘d5 ♕xd2+ 14.♕xd2 cxd5, with compensation:

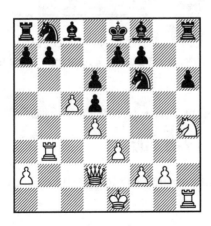

In these kinds of positions with a dynamic balance, Black generally gets the upper hand, since he is, in principle, better prepared for this game!

6...♗g7 7.♘f3 ♛b6?!

An inaccuracy. Only experience can bring an understanding of how the pieces interact with one another in this opening. It turns out that the c3-knight's uncovering the bishop on the queen should not frighten Black, so all I had to do was to complete my development, playing something like ...d7-d6, etc.

8.♛c1 d6 9.e4 h5

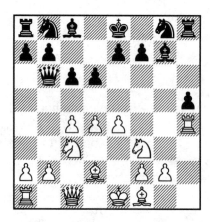

With this move, Black is not so much getting the h-pawn out from under fire as securing the fantastic square g4 for his minor pieces.

9...♗xd4? 10.♘a4 ♗xf2+ 11.♚e2 ♛a6 12.♚xf2 ♛xa4 13.♗c3±.

10.♗e3 ♗g4 11.♗e2 ♘d7

But now it really is time to pick up the d4-pawn – 11...♗xf3!:

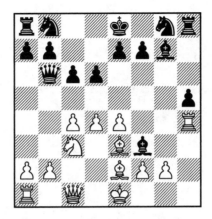

12.♗xf3 ♗xd4 13.♗xd4 ♕xd4.

12.♖b1 ♘f8

12...♗xf3! 13.gxf3 ♗xd4 14.♘a4 ♗xe3 15.♘xb6 ♗xc1 16.♘xa8 ♗g5
17.♖h3 ♘gf6 18.e5 ♘xe5 19.f4 ♗xf4−+.

13.d5 c5 14.b4 ♘d7 15.bxc5 ♕a5

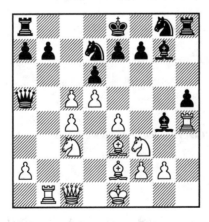

White's position is disorganized. For Black, it's "business as usual" in the Elshad System, while White is unable to resolve the problems that confront him.

16.♗d2

16.♗d4!? ♗xd4 17.♘xd4 ♘xc5 18.f3 (18.♗xg4?? ♘d3+) 18...♘a4.

16...♘xc5 17.♘b5 ♕d8 18.♗c3 ♘f6 19.e5 ♘fe4 20.♘g5 a6

20...♘xg5! 21.♕xg5 ♗h6−+:

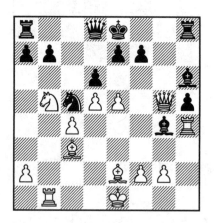

In the jungles of this opening, White's queen frequently gets lost!

21.♘xe4 ♘xe4 22.♗xg4 axb5

22...hxg4! 23.♖xh8+ ♗xh8 24.♕h6 ♗xe5 25.♗xe5 dxe5 26.♘c7+ ♕xc7 27.♕h8+ ♔d7 28.♕xa8 ♕a5+ 29.♔f1 ♘d2+ 30.♔g1 ♘xb1 31.♕xb7+ ♕c7 32.♕xb1 ♕xc4.

23.♗xh5 ♘xc3 24.♗xf7+ ♔xf7 25.♕f4+ ♔g8 26.♖xh8+ ♔xh8 27.♖b3

Pure agony.

27...b4 28.♕f5 ♕g8 29.♖xb4 ♗xe5 30.♖xb7 ♕xg2 31.♖xe7 ♕e4+

31...♕h1+! 32.♔d2 ♕d1+ 33.♔e3 ♕e2#.

32.♕xe4 ♘xe4 33.f4 ♗c3+ 34.♔d1 ♘c5 35.♔c2 ♗f6 0-1

74. K. Tagirov – Elshad

2007

1.b4

The Sokolsky (or Polish) Opening. Well, OK then: let's see how the inventor of the line deals with an opponent who plays original chess himself.

1...d6 2.♗b2

One of the ideas in the Sokolsky is to bring the dark-squared bishop out to b2. , The Elshad System works out quite well to counter this plan: we will block the activity of this fianchettoed bishop with ...d7-d6 and ...e7-e5.

2...♘d7 3.c4 a5!

Strongest. Black's task is to take control of every dark square on the board.

4.b5?!

Surrendering the c5 square. Better is 4.a3!? axb4 5.axb4 ♖xa1 6.♗xa1 c5 7.bxc5 ♘xc5, when we have an original sort of position with equal chances.

4...c6 5.a4 ♘gf6 6.e3 g5!?

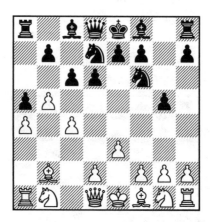

Otherwise this would simply be a Polish. But now Black shows clearly in what sector of the board he intends to play.

7.h3

How often does White, right in the opening, need to take steps to enable his knight to come out to f3?

7...h5 8.d3

8.♘f3 ♖g8!.

8...♕c7 9.♘f3 ♖g8! 10.♗e2

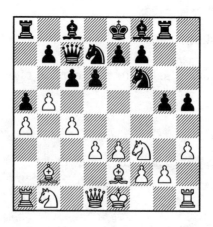

10...e5

The immediate ...g5-g4! deserves close attention: 10...g4!?
11.hxg4 hxg4 12.♘d4 ♘e5 (12...g3!? 13.f4 ♘c5) 13.♘c3 c5 14.♘b3
♗g7. In such positions, White's problems are of a purely psychological nature, for he "has" to hide his king somewhere! Confusion, loss
of energy, weakened resistance, and rage at the opponent: "What
the heck is Black doing?"

11.♘h2

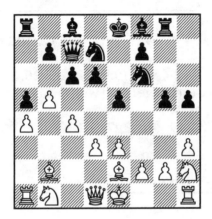

11...e4!?

Now White's head is spinning.

Black can also play 11...♘c5!? 12.d4 exd4 13.exd4 ♘ce4 14.0-0
d5!∓, with a direct and most likely irresistible attack on the white king.

12.dxe4 g4

Bullets are flying in from all directions!

13.hxg4 ♘xe4 14.♗f3

14.gxh5 ♖xg2 15.♘g4 ♘e5 16.♗xe5 ♗xg4 17.♗xg4 dxe5 18.♖a2
(how else to defend the f2 square?) 18...cxb5 19.♗f3 ♕xc4 20.♗xg2
♖d8! 21.♖d2 ♘xd2 22.♘xd2 ♖xd2 23.♔xd2 ♗b4#:

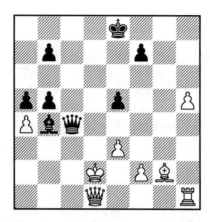

14...d5 15.♗xe4 dxe4 16.♕d4 ♘c5 17.♘d2 f5

17...♘d3+! 18.♔e2 ♘xb2 19.♕xb2 ♗g7 20.♕a2 ♗xa1 21.♕xa1 ♗e6∓. White is the exchange down with an inferior position to boot.

18.0-0-0 ♘d3+ 19.♔b1 ♗g7 0-1

75. G. Guliev – Elshad

2003

1.e4 d6 2.d4 ♘d7 3.♗e3 h6 4.♘c3

Yet another short, cute victory in a game where White omits playing c2-c4. I must remind you that although White's chances are better here, that does not eliminate the opportunity for creative play.

4...c6 5.♗c4 g5 6.♕h5

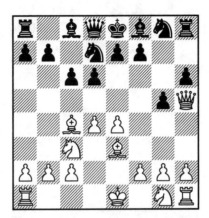

One so wants to play it like this – Scholar's Mate is threatened.

6...♖h7!!

Brilliant!

6...d5!? (there is this possibility as well, with excellent play for Black) 7.exd5 ♘gf6 8.♕e2 cxd5 9.♗xd5 (9.♘xd5?? ♘xd5 10.♗xd5 ♕a5+) 9...♘xd5 10.♘xd5 ♕a5+ 11.♘c3 ♗g7. Black has a wonderful game for a mere pawn.

7.♗xg5? ♕a5! 8.e5 ♘xe5!

This he had to see ahead of time.

9.♗e2

9.dxe5 ♕xe5+ 10.♕e2 ♕xe2+ 11.♘gxe2 hxg5. Black boasts the bishop pair and an extra pawn.

9...hxg5!!

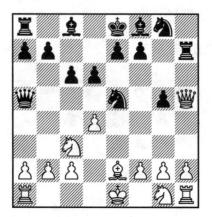

10.♕xh7 ♘f6 11.♕h8 ♘g6

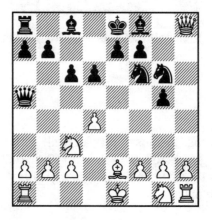

The queen is caught. White resigned.

0-1

76. Lewiseisen – NemtsevIgor

Live Chess on Chess.com 10/13/2015

1.e4 c6 2.d4 d6

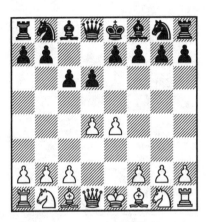

Although this move does give White the better chances in the coming battle, one still wants to try playing the Elshad against 1.e4.

3.♘c3 ♘d7 4.♘f3 h6 5.♗e3

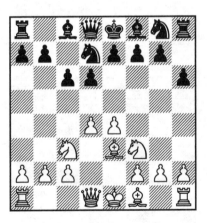

Let's ponder this for a moment. If White expects Black to play ...g7-g5, and wants to meet that with h2-h4 – then this move (♗c1-e3) looks out of place. The bishop could attack the g-pawn just as well from the c1 square. On the other hand, if White is preparing to castle queenside, then he has no need to rush with h2-h4.

5...g5 6.h4

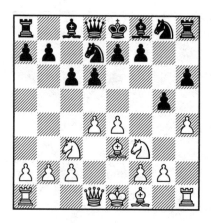

6...g4!

Strongest. One of the main ideas of ...g7-g5 is the advance ...g5-g4 to push the white knight off f3, when the horse will have no decent square to retreat to. In addition, this knight defends d4.

7.♘h2?! h5 8.f3?

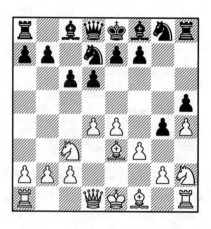

White has "executed" his planned break...

8...g3

...but drops the knight.

0-1

77. Santa11 (2838) – Nemtsev_Igor (2808)

10/13/2015

1.d4 c6 2.c4 d6 3.♘f3 ♘d7 4.♘c3 h6 5.♗f4 g5 6.♗g3 ♗g7 7.e3

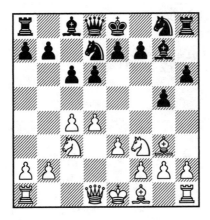

7...h5

White is trying to play the London System, but without taking concrete factors here into account. He runs into a tactical refutation.

8.♘xg5?

8.h4 g4 9.♘d2 ♘f8 leads back into a "normal" position for this opening. However, we should note that castling short here is fraught with dangers for White. The g7-bishop can go to f6 and the knight to g6, when the h4-pawn would be in trouble.

8...h4 9.♗f4 e5 10.dxe5 dxe5

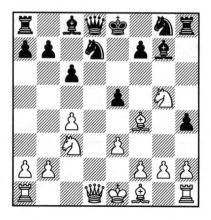

The bishop is trapped.

11.♗e2 exf4 12.exf4 h3 13.♘xh3 ♕b6 14.0-0 ♕xb2 15.♘e4 ♕xa1 16.♕xa1 ♗xa1 17.♖xa1 ♘gf6 18.♘d6+ ♔e7 19.♘f5+ ♔f8 20.♘g5 ♘c5

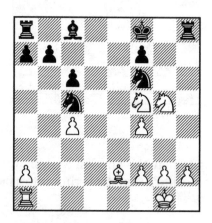

Black is a rook up and the rest of the game lacks interest.

21.♘d6 ♘e6 22.♘gxf7 ♖h7 23.♘g5 ♘xg5 24.fxg5 ♘d7 25.f4 ♘c5 26.f5 ♖d7 27.♖d1 ♔e7 28.f6+ ♔f8 29.g6 ♖xd6 30.♖xd6 ♗f5 31.g7+ ♔f7 32.g4 ♗g6 33.h4 ♖e8 34.♗f3 ♗e4

35.♗d1 ♔g6 36.g5 ♗f5 37.h5+ ♔xg5 38.f7 ♖e1+ 39.♔h2 ♘e4 40.g8♕+ ♔f4 41.♖d4 ♖f1 42.f8♕ ♖f2+ 43.♔g1 ♖g2+ 44.♕xg2 ♔e5 45.♕f3 ♗g4 0-1

78. vakim50 (2339) – Nemtsev_Igor (2733)

3/10/2015

1.♘f3 c6 2.d4 d6 3.♗f4

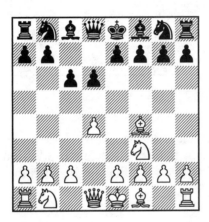

We like this move (for us, that is!). Again, White is playing the London System, but in our setup the dark-squared bishop will become a target.

3...h6 4.h3 g5 5.♗g3

Putting the bishop on h2 is preferable, and standard for positions featuring h2-h3.

5...♗g7 6.e4 ♘d7 7.♗e2 ♕b6

Given that the bishop has departed the queenside, it makes sense to bring out my queen to b6. Generally speaking, if White has not played c2-c4, he retains the chance to play c2-c3, protecting the d4-pawn by natural means. All the more reason, then, to deploy the queen to b6, as we'll soon see.

8.b3

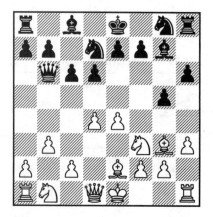

8...c5!

Just so – there's no time for routine moves. The a1-h8 diagonal is practically begging to be opened, and in addition we are attacking the d4-pawn, White's main pillar in this opening.

9.c3 ♘f8

An inaccuracy, even though it is in the spirit of this system. The point is that players of White are approaching the opening in stereotyped fashion. First they try to develop everything and only then do they embark on active operations. In a general sense, this is the correct approach. But the Elshad System requires us to act concretely from the get-go. White could have generated active play with e4-e5; meanwhile, Black himself has a different possibility in 9...cxd4!, e.g. 10.cxd4 h5! 11.♘c3 (forced – if 11.0-0?!, then 11... g4!∓ 12.hxg4 hxg4 13.♘h2 ♕xd4 14.♘d2 ♕xa1 15.♕xa1 ♗xa1 16.♖xa1 ♘df6, and White will not be able to hold the ending) 11...g4 12.hxg4 hxg4 13.♖xh8 ♗xh8 14.♘d5 ♕d8 15.♘d2 ♘gf6=, or 15...♗xd4 16.♖c1 ♔f8 17.♘c4, with compensation for the material.

10.0-0 ♘e6 11.e5!?

Logical: he needs to generate play somewhere.

11...dxe5

This is the more-or-less standard reaction to e4-e5. In most cases, in the Elshad System we should just take any pawn that shows up on e5 or c5. In this regard, I'm reminded of an interview with one of my favorite authors, GM Sergey Shipov. He said that he might be the only person who had ever read his own book, *The Complete Hedgehog*. Well, make that two of us, then! *[Three of us! – Tr.] [OK, make that four – Ed.]* I read it cover to cover, and I wandered with the author through all the little corners of the system.

And by the way, I liked one of Shipov's concepts: that in the Hedgehog, the proper setup is important. If you know which piece ought to stand where, and where it's headed, the variations will grow organically. In this light, the Elshad System is the same way. Knowing 10-15 basic techniques, you can whack opponents a class or so above you.

12.dxe5 h5

Having encountered this opening for the first time ever, White of course is unsure how to proceed – where's Black planning to put his king? The answer is: nowhere! It will stay in the center, personally overseeing its counterpart's destruction.

13.♘bd2 g4 14.♘c4 ♕c7 15.♘h4?!

15.hxg4 hxg4 16.♘h4 ♘h6 17.♕c2 ♗d7 18.♖ad1 ♖d8 19.a4 b6. This was undoubtedly White's best choice. It's just that opening the h-file looks scary.

15...♘h6 16.♕c2 gxh3 17.gxh3 ♘g5 18.♔h2

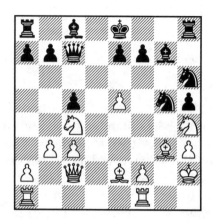

18...♗xh3

18...♕d7! is an unconventional queen maneuver, after which White's chances for a successful defense rapidly drop to zero: 19.♖fd1 ♕xh3+ 20.♔g1 ♗f5 21.♘xf5 ♘xf5 22.♖d3 ♘h4 23.♗xh4 ♕xh4 24.♖g3 ♕f4 25.♖d1 ♔f8.

19.f4 ♗xf1 20.fxg5 ♗xe2?!

20...♘g4+! is much stronger and leads to the win much more quickly: 21.♗xg4 ♗xc4 22.♗h3 ♗xe5 23.♖g1 ♗d5 24.c4 ♗xg3+ 25.♖xg3 ♗c6−+.

21.gxh6 ♗xh6 22.♕xe2 0-0-0 23.e6 ♗f4 24.♕g2 ♖hg8 25.exf7 ♖xg3 26.f8♕ ♖xg2+ 27.♔xg2 ♖xf8 28.♖f1 ♖g8+ 0-1

In Conclusion

And so, this book draws to a close. Of course, your author hopes that this will be just the first edition. My thinking is that if the system grows in popularity, then we can publish a new collection of best games by masters and others in subsequent editions. Since the time I began work on this book, hundreds of new games have been played in blitz and rapid chess – not just by your author, but by Elshad himself and by many others who already like this opening. If Elshad and I have managed to blaze new trails for you, then we're very happy! There are so many tasty delights in chess! And so, onward and upward! Take up the Elshad System, and you will be guaranteed the occasional victory over masters and grandmasters... at least in rapids or blitz!

About the Author

FIDE Master Igor Evgenievich Nemtsev studied at the Chelyabinsk State Institute of Physical Culture (Chess Division) and has worked as a trainer for 25 years. His students include numerous players of all strengths, including dozens of Candidate Masters, 4 FIDE Masters, and one International Master. In 2000, he was one of the winners (tied for 1st-4th) of the qualifier for the Russian Championship in the city of Vyatskiye Polyany. Currently, he works on chess training and educational activities in person and over the Internet, including children's classes and webinars.

The author's website is: nemtsevChess.com